THE WINCHESTER TALES

AN ANGLO-NORMAN STORY OF LOVE AND DECEIT

The final part of *The Ridge Trilogy*

Translated and edited by Chris Heal
author of *The Four Marks Murders* and *Ropley's Legacy*

From the private papers of
Gilbert of Bayeux, later Gilbert of Ropley

D1344056

Published by Chattaway and Spottiswood
Four Marks, Hampshire
www.candspublishing.org.uk
chrisheal@candspublishing.org.uk

The moral right of Chris Heal to be identified as the author and compiler of
this work has been asserted.
This is a work of historical fact. The names, characters and quotes of the
principal characters, businesses, events and incidents are based on research
which is in the public domain.
Opinions about these events, characters and organisations, unless
specifically attributed, are the views of the author.
Supported by Ropley History Network & Archive.

A catalogue record for this book is available from
the British Library.

5 4 3 2 1

ISBN 978-1-9161944-4-1

Designed and typeset: Mary Woolley, www.battlefield-design.co.uk
Cover design and maps: Paul Hewitt, www.battlefield-design.co.uk
Translations: Brooke Westcott & author
Index: Holly Fletcher
Print liaison and website: Andy Severn, www.oxford-ebooks.com
Print on Demand: www.ingramspark.com

Nothing has ever happened in the villages around here.

Two young men at the *Castle of Comfort*, Medstead, 2019

… the western states suffered great disasters. On the death of those excellent kings, Henry of France and Edward of England, the French and English had long reason to lament their loss, as the princes who succeeded were little like them for virtue and gentleness of disposition. When these fathers of their country were removed, they were followed by tyrants who abused the royal authority. England, stained by the cruelties and perjury of Harold, fell to decay, and deprived of its race of native kings, became a prey to foreign adventurers, the adherents of William the Conqueror, presenting a melancholy subject for the pen of the feeling historian.

Orderic Vitalis, *The Ecclesiastical History*, Book IV, p. 1, c. 1141

The Norman Conquest supplied a point of interest and identification for almost any point of view and this explains the variety of the problems and the difficulty of resolving them. Those who believe that battles can decisively alter history point to Hastings, while those who think change comes slowly and imperceptibly can argue that the battle by itself had little effect. Similarly those who favour authority and military discipline can recognise these traits in the Normans, while liberals and democrats feel some kinship for the Anglo-Saxons. National sentiments can likewise be used in a variety of guises. The Normans are either the oppressors of the English nation and language or its revivifiers. Although the Normans may not have recognised themselves in some of these guises, they would no doubt have been pleased that an interest was still being taken in them a thousand years later, as they liked to be noticed and intended to be remembered.

M. T. Clanchy, *England and its Rulers*, p. 52, 1983

CONTENTS

LIST OF ILLUSTRATIONS

LIST OF MAPS

AUTHOR'S NOTE

The pages of Gilbert of Bayeux's manuscript were discovered in 2021 wound in some scraps of early rent rolls in a chest in the attic of a private house in Ropley. The rolls themselves were badly damaged, almost unreadable. They had no discernible connection with Gilbert's life other than they likely concerned land lying along what later became known as Gilbert Street. From much later rent lists in the Hampshire archives, Gilbert Street was the probable location of Gilbert's home, and his beehives, at the beginning of the twelfth century.

The manuscript contains sixty-seven sheets of calf skin of varying sizes all but three covered in Gilbert's meticulous handwriting. The three extra sheets are letters in two different hands that were written by or for Lēofric (of whom much is told later) during his journey to Jerusalem on pope Urban's crusade.

The text is in Latin, Norman French and, towards the end, in Anglo-Saxon or early English. Gilbert switched often from one to the other as suited the contacts and experiences he described. I have translated in a modern style while seeking to maintain the essential rhythm of Gilbert's prose. As an aid to understanding, I have standardised the names of the places and people mentioned to the current variant. Gilbert made a few, now obvious, errors, confused names mostly, which I have corrected without notification. The arrangement of the chapters is my own choice as are the supporting newly-drawn maps and the selection of illustrations.

For readers who may lose track of some of the various historical characters introduced by Gilbert, I have collected the cast together at the very end of the book in a people index.

I would like to thank the small team of language experts who improved my first translations. I would also like to thank the house owner who brought the manuscript to my attention and requested my interest and my confidence.

Gilbert's story is remarkable. It begins about 1050 with his early life in Bayeux as an orphan servant of Odo, bishop of that city. Gilbert's organisational and language skills saw him called to England in 1067 to form part of the new Norman administration in the old Anglo-Saxon capital of Winchester. Almost always an outsider, he nevertheless witnessed or took part in many of the great local events of the Anglo-Norman era and met most of their protagonists.[1] During this time, he also found the great love of his life, Ailgifu, in Medstead. Their family was born in Winchester. Gilbert died, presumably in Ropley, before 1120. His trenchant and sometimes controversial views are his own and are, therefore, potentially flawed. However, these were his times.

For those who wish to see the events of *The Winchester Tales* in context, I have included a brief chronology of Gilbert's life at the end of his story.

On a personal note, I did not seek out this book. A chance encounter some years ago with two young men in the *Castle of Comfort* public house in Medstead disturbed me. The men claimed nothing of note had ever happened in the locality. It seemed to me that the complete reverse was true. The ridge that blocked the natural river route from London via the northern Wey and the Itchen to Winchester was a piece of country of great interest and history.

In response, in 2020, I wrote a popular social history of the area that became, in 1932, the parish of Four Marks. It concentrated, at least on the surface, on local murders through the ages. To my surprise, *The Four Marks Murders* was a commercial success. The following year, I wrote *Ropley's Legacy*, a history book, which told the dreadful but exciting story of the impoverishment of the local peasantry by land enclosure in the eighteenth and nineteenth centuries. The book concerned the parishes along the ridge: Ropley, Medstead, Farringdon, Chawton and Newton Valence. *Ropley's Legacy*, supported by a grant from the Hampshire Archives Trust, was 'straight' history and received strong critical reviews and moderate sales.

This third book, *The Winchester Tales*, becomes by luck the last in a trilogy that, hopefully, has brought a great deal of new interest to an area with a seemingly unknown past. Gilbert's manuscript can now also take its rightful place as a principal source for the great medieval chronicle written by Orderic Vitalis.

I lost my verbal battle with the two young men in the pub in Medstead a few years ago. Perhaps, now, I can claim to have won the war.

Chris Heal
Four Marks
October, 2022

---

1 Anglo-Norman: After the conquest in 1066, the victorious Normans formed a ruling class in Britain distinct from the native populations, although often intermarrying. The new aristocrats comprised a combination of ethnic Normans, French, Anglo-Saxons, Flemings and Bretons. Over time, a distinct Anglo-Norman language evolved which was used in administration, the courts, schools and universities. Anglo-Norman became, to a large extent, the spoken language of the higher social strata in medieval England.

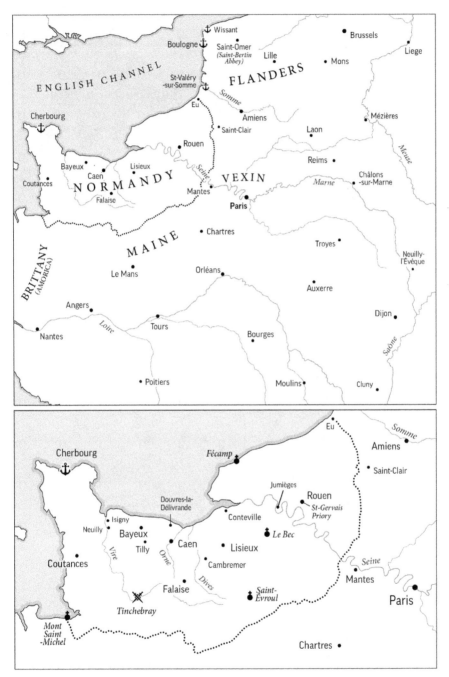

Abbey   **Port**   **Battle site**   ⋯ **Boundary of Normandy**

Map 1: Gilbert's view of Norman France, 1067-1110

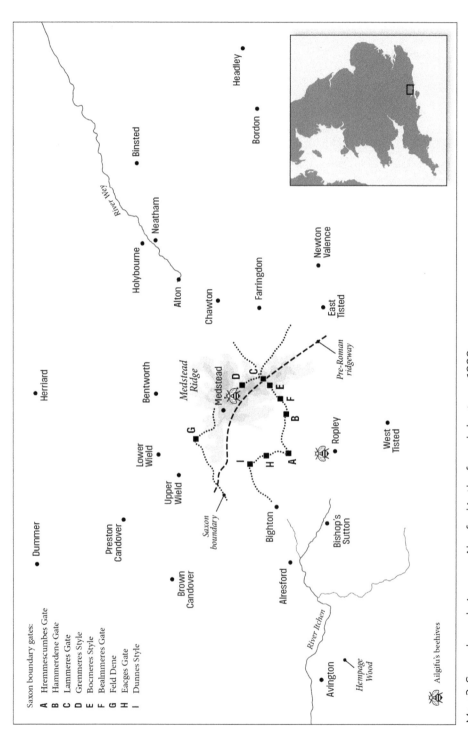

Map 2: Saxon boundaries near Alresford in the forged charter, c. 1090

Saxon boundary gates:

A Hremmescumbes Gate
B Hammerdene Gate
C Lammeres Gate
D Grenmeres Style
E Bocmeres Style
F Bealmmeres Gate
G Feld Dene
H Eacges Gate
I Dunnes Style

Headley

Binsted

Bordon

River Wey

Neatham

Holybourne

Newton
Valence

Alton

Chawton

Farringdon

East
Tisted

Herriard

Bentworth

Medstead
Ridge

Medstead

D

C

E

F

B

Ropley

West
Tisted

Pre-Roman
ridgeway

Dummer

Lower
Wield

G

I

H

A

Preston
Candover

Upper
Wield

Saxon
boundary

Bighton

Bishop's
Sutton

Brown
Candover

Alresford

River Itchen

Avington

Hempage
Wood

Ailgifu's beehives

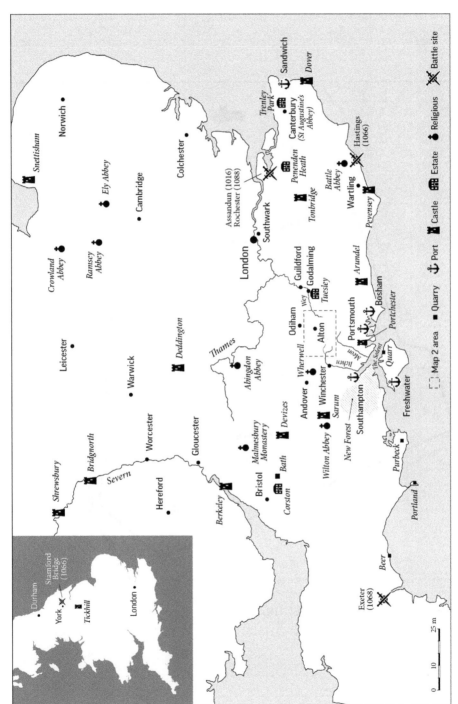

Map 3: Gilbert's view of Norman England, 1067-1110

11

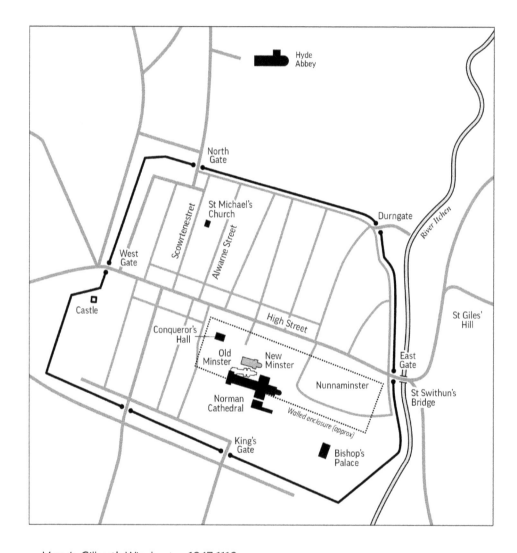

Map 4: Gilbert's Winchester, 1067-1110

PREFACE

THE TASK, 1087: WINCHESTER

'Do you truly believe in God as taught by the holy church in Rome?'

Prosperity, happiness, even safety, hang on such lonely moments. The reply was a heart beat too slow but, when it came, was fulsome and clear.

'With all my being and with each waking thought, my Lord.'

The bishop, hooded eyelids almost closed in a deeply lined face, beaked, veined nose raised, had long experience of men and their shades of commitment. His current eminence was founded on nuance, on binding servants and adversaries while leaving himself the greater freedom. The heart beat had not gone unnoticed. What did it signify? A confused soul? A rebellious spirit? Perhaps a mirror of himself, a threat in years to come?

Walkelin leaned hard on his stick and looked down to where the supplicant's face was half-covered by a black cowl. As always, he followed instinct.

'And under my guidance, Gilbert of Bayeux, before all others except only the king?'

Gilbert understood the explicit commitment that was required, the change of master, the loss of independence. If he wished to advance his prospects, it was too late to seek an alternative. He had chosen to sup in public with the devil in white ermine and crimson satin.

'Above all others, my Lord.'

Feet shuffled discreetly around the room as the bishop's retinue watched for any hint of rejection. The oak panels with their Christian draperies were impassive; the long tapestries that lauded Norman victories at arms fell lifeless in the summer heat; the open windows brought faint, tired cries of Winchester's street mongers. Two bluebottles buzzed without a pattern, impertinent and purposeless.

After a long, slow minute, Walkelin called Gilbert to his feet and offered his episcopal ring, the signal of acceptance and obeisance, of a life-deal struck.

Gilbert pecked the dull emerald clasped in silver.

'I have a task for you.' Walkelin coughed, dry-mouthed. An acolyte rushed forward with wine. 'It requires energy and discretion which, I hear, you provide in plenty. You will need to employ many of the skills taught you by the traitorous Lord Odo and his servants.'

Walkelin lowered, but intensified, his voice, and fixed Gilbert's eyes. 'Your success is necessary to the future of my holy jurisdiction at Winchester and, therefore, to my new cathedral and to the glory of God. My chosen men do not fail me.'

He raised a small jewelled finger and a steward stepped forward, head inclined, and spread an arm towards a heavy, studded door. Gilbert bowed deeply, ended the audience and followed his guide. He would soon hear what immoral deed his new master needed done.

1 ODO AND THE COMET, 1050-1066

There was a self-congratulatory joke much shared in Norman communities in the last quarter of the eleventh century: no matter who was asked in the Christian territories of Europe all could remember where they were and who they were with when they first heard that William the Bastard had smashed the English army. King Harold was dead, hacked to pieces by three knights while wounded, in a battle that stunned established and unshockable rulers.

With the papal banner of approval flying over the invaders at Hastings, the event highlighted the gospel of Norman military superiority and proved William's God-given and rightful claim to the throne. And all of which, I slowly came to learn, was a myth, nurtured, embellished, and turned into accepted truth, yet a myth all the same.

I was given the name Gilbert, not another bastard I thought, but at least an orphan. My unknown parents were cut down before me in a forgotten village somewhere on the border with Maine. I could never recall their faces. My captors took me, a snivelling boy about five years old, to work in the kitchens of my Lord Odo's palace at Bayeux which stood within the Roman walls. Odo of Conteville was recently given the position by his half-brother, duke William, while still in his teens. For the first year, I never saw the new bishop, but word of his casual brutality was daily fare among the pots, pans and greasy water. A smudge mark on a soup bowl would be enough, the table stewards assured me, for my worthless body to be spitted and carefully roasted. The cooks discussed the best sauce to complement my seared flesh. In the early hours of each morning, I would slump into a corner with some scraps of straw dotted with rat droppings and sob myself to sleep.

When my Lord was at home and the main hall was full of hungry, drunken men, the augmented staff in the great kitchen ranges seemed to come from all parts of the Norman empire. I picked up the various tongues, assimilated nuance and slang, and slipped with ease from one to another. Aged ten, I was asked to carry and to translate orders from the chefs to their workers. Soon, I joined the meeting at the central table where daily menus were discussed, work allocated and standards set. My opinion was never required, but I was expected to tour the preparation and cooking rooms ready with answers. My evidence was frequently called when punishments for poor work were allocated. Language gave me power. Scrubbing dishes was soon no longer my concern.

My quick tongue found its way to the great hall and I was taught to wait on foreign dignitaries and especially sisters and female cousins married to distant noble families. Seeing my Lord Odo for the first time, I was grateful that I was kept away from his hands. He seemed very young, but his temper flashed before thought and was mountainous. Often, deep hurt was done to a passing innocent. I realised that a bishop, while serving God, could be committed to the delights of the flesh, a slave to worldly trivialities. Everyone knew of his mistress. He was always surrounded by youths, foppish with silk garments and bold colours who wore their hair longer than necessary. My kitchen masters warned me to keep my head lowered and to wear my clothes loose otherwise I might find myself spitted in another way.

Always at table, if slightly distant from the more boisterous revels, visiting Benedictine monks from Odo's bare construction site of a cathedral and his churches in the villages around, watched with disapproval. I asked one day what language they used to share their opinions and so I was introduced to Latin. One monk, a poet called Serlo, gained permission for me to join his small early morning class at the monastery just outside the town walls. Caen and Bayeux had begun to thrive on the trade that followed Normandy's new-found stability. Wherever there was good trade in the province, monasteries were sure to follow. Whatever his sinful personal habits, my Lord Odo was lauded for using his wealth and power to enrich the church and to encourage the identification and development of young clerks to provide the empire's backbone of clear communication.

For several days, I gazed wide-eyed at scraps of parchment presented by Serlo, the lines neat, minuscule, symmetrical and never-ending. Wayward flecks floated above and below without meaning. Serlo recited with barely a glance at each sheet, telling stories of the Almighty. Through a haze, I saw no connection between speech and squiggle. I remember the moment when the haze shifted in a warm breeze, forms swayed, became shapes, drifted away and came back stronger. Suddenly, I realised that all was connected. I knew with clarity that all answers were before me and that I would become master of these thin lines of knowledge. I railed against going back to the kitchen. I begged to be allowed to take some scraps of vellum to decipher. I found chalk and worked copies on brick walls.

One day, Serlo ruffled my hair and gave me my first quill and black ink and some well used stretches of skin with patches of bare space.

'Do good in the service of your Lord,' was all he said. He took me to Thurstin, a parish priest with a boisterous family, to further my studies each afternoon. I was often called on to lull the youngest son, Ranulf, to sleep. [*He was a future bishop in England, an opportunist, a brilliant organiser, as incendiary as Odo and a downright thief. Some fifty years later, we sat opposite each other in a tent in Hampshire where, for a few minutes, we held the future of the crown in our hands.*][1]

Under Thurstin's instruction, the jumps from Latin to Norman to French to Breton were soon small steps. I understood their purpose and devoured the differences. His burgeoning school introduced the *trivium*, rhetoric, dialectic and grammar, and the *quadrivium*, arithmetic, geometry, music and astronomy; his intellectual reflections dwelt on the exercise of power and on respect for archives. Within a month of translating numbers and discovering tabulation, I sat for an hour at most morning kitchen tables and produced lists of the ingredients needed for that day. I moved from kitchen inventory to establish agreed food prices, to anticipate wastage and to suggest to Geoffrey, bishop Odo's chamberlain, how best to deal with suppliers.

Thurstin began to despair. What he sought from me were manuscripts with lavishly coloured display capitals of winding serpents and curling foliage that would glorify the word of God. What he got were tools for managing a household.

He looked down at me with reproachful eyes.

'God has not yet spoken to your heart,' he said and waited for my tears of dismay. Disappointed at my silence, he continued, 'You will not become a novice, nor will you go to the episcopal school at Laon as I had hoped. You are to become a clerk in the service of my Lord the bishop. You will be expected to write the

---

1   The text is contemporaneous throughout with a handful of minor exceptions, placed by the editor in italics within square brackets, to indicate mostly where Gilbert had returned to his script to add a later comment or, less often, to identify an intrusion into the story for clarity.

letters and charters in the ducal household. You must be accurate, honest and obedient. Perhaps your lord will recognise and reward you. Follow me.'

We traced our way past the heart of the bishop's residence to a corridor lined down one side by identical oak doors. Thurstin opened one.

'This is your room,' he told me with a sigh. He placed his hands on my shoulders, kissed my forehead and handed me an elaborate carved wooden pen case in an Anglo-Saxon style. My name was inscribed on the underside of its head. [*I did not recognise it then, but it was the beginning of a life-long obsession with things English.*] Thurstin turned and left and I never saw him again.

I looked about and half-believed I was in heaven. The walls were well covered in white plaster. High on one side was a window with glass, a material I had only ever touched in religious places. Facing was a large cross. I saw a bed with its fine and fresh straw paillasse and pillow. To one side was a stool and rough table where I placed the pen case, my first possession. In the corner, breeches and a tunic sporting a large gold cross were laid out on a chest. I was already marked as Odo's man.

I spent several minutes moving from stool to bed then gazing outside to racing, grey clouds above green and brown field strips where men worked and cattle lay down ready for rain. My door opened. An older boy stood dressed in a tunic which matched mine. He inspected me briefly and ordered me to follow without questions.

'You are to be tested,' he explained, 'to see if you are as good as the priest claims.'

The room was windowless and uninviting. I stood where I was told facing a long trestle table. It was covered in plain cloth with goblets and wine and water jugs for the five men who stared at me. My guide closed the door and stood as if on guard. No one spoke for fully five minutes.

'I am Thomas. Do you believe in God?' asked a thin man. He had a pock-marked face framed by a monk's black robe held with a pristine white rope. He spoke in Latin, the language of culture and the work tool of clerks.

I replied that I did. It was the only answer, of course, although I was already old enough to know that in spite of the church's all pervasiveness, most people were not especially pious. Normandy was a society of saints and sinners who often inhabited the same man. The papacy was a feeble institution in the middle of the eleventh century with little real authority and which scarcely ever intervened in the decisions of local churches. When the papacy did begin to assert its authority, the change sent shock waves through western political society.

Another monk, in French, ordered me to explain my reasons. Then, in Norman with its bastardised Danish from the end of the table, 'Is bishop Odo your Lord?' In Breton, 'Describe your cell.'

Finally, a question in a tongue I did not know. I replied in Norman, 'I apologise, my Lord, I believe you have spoken to me in English. I cannot answer you. It is a language I would like to learn.'

A man in ornate clothing and wearing a short sword pushed an illuminated manuscript toward me and told me to read. It was the *Lord's Prayer*. When I had finished, he asked what I thought of the transcription.

'There is a mistake in the third line,' I said. ' I substituted the correct word.'

He pushed materials across the table. 'Write what you had for breakfast.' When I had finished and he had read my words, he signalled for my guide to take me away.

'Go to your cell and pray,' he instructed as I passed through the door. A pause, then, 'You have done well.'

The next day I was given a donkey and told to learn how to look after it and to ride. When I returned to my cell there was a pile of manuscript sheets on my table. There was no explanation, no order and the writing was in many hands and mistake-ridden. The sheets constituted the rent records of bishop Odo's local estates. I began work: two hours in the morning and an hour in the early evening with my animal named, well there is no easy translation, but 'grunt' is probably best to describe his constant complaint at being put to effort; and, the rest, meals apart, at deciphering my records. In the kitchen, I usually ate alone and saw an unexpected deference in the eyes of the child waiters. They were wary of my clumsy attempts at joviality.

I realised that Odo was very rich; his lands could have supported three bishops. As well as the palace, Odo had large houses at Caen, Lisieux and Rouen. There was a castle at Neuilly l'Évêque and fortified manors at Douvres-la-Délivrande and Cambremer. Within these estates, there were many tenant craftsmen charged with developing commercial activity. Odo would gain from the tolls paid on the traffic of goods to his markets and fairs held in churchyards at Neuilly, Isigny, Plessis, St Clair, St Vigor-le-grand, Tilly and Cambremer.

Among the mess of the rent records, the estate that bothered me most was that of Neuilly. Its three castles and two mottes and baileys lorded over a dozen settlements that were scattered between the rivers Vire and Elle and contained many salt pans, three mills at best count and two large fishponds. To the east, an extensive deer park and forest added hunting ground to others tracts near Bayeux. After a week of research and note taking, I was summoned to the chamberlain to explain how I was going to improve my Lord Bishop's income. I respected Geoffrey's sharp mind, but was confused by his sparrow eyes which darted everywhere and never settled. It was a conversation full of twists and unfinished sentences on both our parts.

I said I would like to start by visiting Neuilly because there was no pattern in the rents received. It was made clear that I would have no authority to set or collect rents, but only to report. I pointed out that I did not know where Neuilly was and that I was worried about how I would be treated especially if there were problems. A parchment of authority was pushed across the table. It was a fair and open statement of my mission. A serjeant-at-arms and three mounted squires were to direct and protect me.

'I have also asked Adam fitz Hubert, the youngest brother of Eudo Dapifer, the duke's steward, to go with you. He knows Neuilly from the hunt and will, no doubt, take some of his own men. Adam is about your age and will prove useful to you if you can make your mark with him. He is there only to provide advice.'

Details of the estate's status were evaded, especially when I asked about hunting rights.

'Bishops are prohibited by church law from hunting,' offered the chamberlain. 'However, aristocrats are not. My Lord Odo's brother, the duke William, loves deer as he loved his father.' He paused and then explained that, likewise, bishops were not allowed to marry and, therefore, other 'arrangements' were treated by papal Rome with dismay. 'Even now, Odo expects to be succeeded by a son,' he said. 'There will be a reckoning.'

His argument leapt. 'I mention the duke William because there is a great venture afoot that will change all our lives, yours included. I hope under God's grace that it will be for the better. Your bishop wishes to be the foremost supporter of his brother in his endeavour and needs to raise his revenues. Your success in Neuilly is a part of this plan.'

I wondered whether to delve further as an invasion of England was everywhere discussed in quiet corners. The opportunity was lost.

'Come and see me in two weeks with a solution at Neuilly. And bring a map.' I was dismissed.

The next morning, late, my group of ten set off heading west. My plodding donkey with wooden writing table flapping in the wind followed nine finely mounted warriors. A large sack hung at my side with the old records and new parchment and materials to record what I was to find. After less than ten minutes, just outside the city wall at Vaucelles, Adam stopped at an inn. He sent one of his men back to town, called for drinks and ordered me to sit with him.

'I shall go mad with boredom with your damn donkey,' he said. 'Do you go to England?'

I shook my head in wonder at his directness.

'My father and brothers are upset. We have been asked to stay to protect our ports against the Danes. We shall miss out on all the fighting and the booty. My father is pressing that we be allowed to go in the early reserves. The glory will be less, of course.'

Adam asked if I knew much of our history, assuming that I was born into the great Norman hegemony.

'Very little,' I replied. 'My time has been spent learning practical things to serve my Lord Odo's interests.'

He gave me a sideways look and launched into one of his favourite sagas as the men gathered around. They were delighted by histories. The Norman leaders needed to have their exploits recorded by chroniclers who developed an enduring record of their deeds. What Adam told me was important, although jumbled, and clearly followed the preferred truth, but the real benefit to me was that scales fell from my eyes. I realised that with practice I could tell his stories in much better fashion and that with stories lay information and in their presentation lay another route to power through influence.

When the Romans invaded Britain a thousand year ago, said Adam, there was a great increase in commerce with Gaul. Also, there was a southward movement of British people escaping from Roman dominance into western Armorica where they settled and gave it the name of Brittany. Then the Saxons came across the sea from the north and the Romans left. They were supposedly Trojans who fled following the sack of Troy or from Alexander the Great's army who were in turn descended from the followers of Priam and settled in Macedonia.

'Our ancestors began to plunder along the coast of Flanders during the reign of Charlemagne,' said Adam, warming to his task and pleased with the rapt faces of the listeners.

At first, the Danes and 'heathen men' attacked Britain and Ireland. By the middle of the ninth century, they raided along the coasts of Gaul. Sailing up rivers, they struck inland. In 841, Rouen and Jumièges were burnt; an expedition in 845 reached Paris. Attacks on Brittany were fought off, but in 851 the invaders wintered for the first time on the lower Seine. As they threatened the monasteries, relics were carried inland for safety.

Adam switched to the first person to entrap his audience.

'We made allies among the Bretons. On the Loire, we penetrated to Angers, Chartres, Tours, Orléans. In 1003, we Danes were given free use of harbours to dispose of loot gathered in England. The Norman dukes accepted Christianity with its principle of monogamy, but Danish custom was still vigorous enough for their bastard sons to enjoy almost full acceptance.

'After Cnut conquered England in 1016, everything became a mess of nationalities. The two lands shared a common Scandinavian heritage. Danes were everywhere; Saxons were everywhere. Intermarriage was common among the ruling families. Emma, sister to duke Richard II of Normandy, wed the English king Æthelred the Unready. Æthelred's children, including Edward the Confessor, were left behind when the parents went back to England, Æthelred to death and Emma to marry Cnut.'

And here, Adam was cut short as his rider returned with a spare horse. The reins were handed to me.

'This is more befitting your position as an emissary of my Lord Bishop,' Adam said. 'You can keep it until you have no more need of it. I appreciate a good listener. The serjeant will follow with the donkey. I suspect chamberlain Geoffrey will want to see the damn beast accounted for. And, we can get a move on to Neuilly before dusk.'

Adam sent two of his men ahead as, over the next five hours, we made steady progress while I learned the ways of my independent horse called *Thor*. Our welcome was respectful if wary and was helped considerably by Adam's presence. The next morning, after making sure I would meet the right people, he retired with his men to *La Maison du Pas* which adjoined the park woodland. He would hunt until I called for his favour.

I do not need to recount my twenty-five meetings, all full of evasion and confusion. What was evident was that the lower orders were squeezed for every sou and the higher the rank of the household the less likely was any full payment whether in money, produce or knightly service. I was threatened or berated each day, but once my accusers knew that every word was noted and every agreement or rent written down, negotiations were soon offered. The style of my arrival with Adam, now waiting in the wings though never called, meant reasonableness was in the air. There was a deep fear of the bishop and whatever punishments he might mete out for past offences.

Ten days of intensive riding gave me a surprising affection for *Thor*. His keep was a preoccupation. I never saw the donkey again. I was able to talk to Adam as we rode back to Bayeux. He gave his views on the success of Norman dynastic management. At all times, he explained, the distinguishing feature of the Normans was allegiance to a leader, not ethnic unity. People applauded the first counts for successfully welding diverse elements into a single people; a process which during expansion was honed in the countries where they settled.

'Because we have a short history in this land, we are not above rewriting events to establish a spurious antiquity,' he admitted with a smile. 'Warfare is the national business of the Norman and hunting our fervent leisure. It is as fighting men that we are praised and remembered with admiration as well as hated by our enemies.

'My father tells his sons that we must be generous to the church. We cannot rule without the bishops. Working with the local church makes us more acceptable to the indigenous population. Then, when we firmly enforce just laws we try never to act as tyrants.

'Anyone can join us. There is no class or ethnic barrier to a military career. All young men master the bow and arrow when hunting. We switched from boats with raiders to mounted men expert in lance, javelin and sword. And we can control our horses.'

He danced his horse around me in a series of disciplined manoeuvres to make his point. He was very good and was quickly joined by his men who delighted in showing their joint skills.

At Bayeux, I was summoned to Geoffrey the morning after my return. He was impatient and eager. I showed him my lists of properties, their tenants and their payments all supported by a map which had taken me a day's labour. The chamberlain had a number of suggestions on accuracy, but, in truth, added little. That afternoon I was at table with my Lord Bishop, at first nervous, but quickly in charge of the report as I realised that my parchments held the power. After an hour, Odo exploded and began detailing the severity of his response to his 'deceitful' tenants. Blinding and castration were high on the list. There was indeed a vengeful and vicious man within his splendid bishop's attire.

I waited for a gap which came when he grappled with thoughts of further hurts he could employ.

'There is another way, my Lord, which might commend itself to you. Used carefully it could meet your needs without the bother of disturbing all your relationships.'

Odo glowered at me for my impertinence and denial of his heinous pleasures. Geoffrey shifted on his seat and lowered his eyes believing I had gone too far. Odo was red above his beard and I could see his struggle to contain his anger.

'Gilbert,' he said at last, 'because of the good you have done, I will give you space, but do not try me further.'

'My Lord,' I replied, bowing, 'I offer simple thoughts for your embellishment and for your greater glory.' Adam had recommended just the right level of obsequiousness.

I explained my plan. There was one man who had been consistently rude to me during my investigation. He held a manor at St Lambert which managed many of the salt pans. It was clear he had carefully misreported their output and value. His foul treatment of his workers and their families was a matter of regular report.

'Make one example of him quickly with devastating punishment,' I suggested and paused, 'to encourage the others. Then, let it be known that you will be the foremost in the support of your brother's venture to claim his rightful throne. You will decide which of your tenants will be permitted to follow you. The best of those who have made fitting contributions in money or in fighting men that result from letters that I will draw up will be allowed to join the expedition. They will became rich if they are courageous and loyal and survive. They will have a different life from those you do not choose.

'I expect my visits to your other manors will be quick and profitable.'

Geoffrey's mouth was open. His eyes darted everywhere. Odo looked at me squarely for a full minute.

'Geoffrey,' he ordered, 'we will have to keep a sharp eye on this young man. I want him close by me. Make his suggestions happen. And crucify that salty traitor. I want to hear his torment all the way from Neuilly.'

He turned to me. 'Let me know if your grand plan meets my needs.'

Nine months later, on the Tuesday after Easter, I was summoned one evening to the roof of the bishop's palace where my Lord Odo had ordered the best wine and a roasted pig. I never wore my finest clothes in front of the bishop; I knew my lowly status and wanted Odo to know that I knew it. However, I did have a private library to work on my records. It was within the quickly growing cathedral of Notre Dame with its stunning and unique ribbed vaulting in the towers. My new cell was three times larger than before. I had two servants and three horses in the stables at my manor of St Lambert. I stood near the bishop, but not close, for only exalted company was allowed. These were the willing contributors to Odo's gift to his brother. Apart from 200 boats being quickly built behind the sweeping sandbanks at the mouth of the River Dives near Caen, 120 fully-equipped knights, six times the number required, were pledged through Odo to William. Despite all the expense, the bishop's treasure chests were full. I had been right: my inquisitions into the episcopal estate had been short, to the point and profitable.

While the magnificence of the cathedral was plain in sight to the north, this was not the reason for the gathering on the palace roof. Conversation was slight and heads were turned upwards. Above was a fearsome thing, an omen, with a light that almost equalled the moon. A comet star had punched across the sky for ten days now trailing its long flaming hair, four times the size of Venus. The nameless star portended, as all learned men knew, a change in government, a result that always followed its previous appearances every 75 years. As Odo announced that night, its arrival coupled with the news of a papal blessing, meant certainty for William's great expedition planned for a few months' time.

[*As I read later, the star was witnessed in a monastery in Malmesbury in England by a old monk called Æthelmær who crouched in terror as he wrote:*

You've come, you source of tears to many mothers. It is long since I saw you;
but as I see you now you are much more terrible, for I see you brandishing the
downfall of my country.]

The fleet moved up the coast to St-Valéry-sur-Somme in Ponthieu. Some men drowned in the transfer, but their loss was kept secret to keep morale high. William boarded his flagship, *Mora*, which his wife, Matilda, had given him from her own funds. Matilda stayed and governed Normandy in William's absence. By reputation, she was a formidable lady, but I never met her.

Adam and I gathered with many other men from Bayeux and Rouen to watch Odo leave with William on an evening in late September. I counted almost 750 square-rigged ships with cruciform banners at their mastheads and a carved lion's head at each prow, and an estimated 7,000 men and 2,000 horses. Among the armour and weapons, some vessels carried bags of metal pins and ready-cut wooden beams for quick castle construction on top of thrown up earthworks. We heard later that most of the boats landed unopposed at Pevensey at dawn. The first action taken on English soil was to seize livestock, slaughter it with battle axes, roast it on spits and serve it in a banquet presided over by Odo. The next action was to lay waste to some twenty villages around Hastings.

The usurper Harold Godwinson, whom some called king, rushed his core army on horseback from the Stamford Bridge in the north where he had just defeated and killed Harald Hardrada, the king of Norway, and his own traitorous brother, Tostig, earl of Northumbria.

The core of Harold's force were crack troops, but his tired army was by no means complete, many left behind without horses. His new force was made up of hastily assembled local militia mixed with little trained and poorly armed villagers. William moved to meet Harold near Hastings and gave the tired English troops no respite on Senlac Hill above the settlement. It was a grim, day-long battle with heavy casualties and ascendancy moved back and forwards.

William led from the front as a warrior king with three horses killed under him. Odo thundered in the rear waving his mace to encourage repeated charges, not being allowed as a bishop to fight. He claimed from his horse that a leader 'should be as gentle as a lamb to good men and to the obedient and humble, but as harsh as a lion to law breakers'. Of course, I had seen the real Odo who gleefully accepted my suggested human sacrifice at the salt pans of Neuilly.

Only an error caused the English to break the security of their shield wall and rush down the hill to their own slaughter at the hands of the Norman cavalry. Harold and his brothers, Gyrth and Leofwine, died and were buried on the beach in mockery for their theft of William's rightful crown. Other English bodies were left as they fell in disgrace until gathered up by local people days later.

When I heard of the great vindication that was to change my life, I was sitting on my own in a corner of the cathedral with a plate of lamb, fresh bread and a large glass of wine. The news was brought to me by an excited young man who burbled for a few minutes then rushed off to share with whoever he could find.

Myth-makers soon took over, but the victory, decisive on the field, was by no means a clear cut end to the war which continued for several years. [*Sadly, I was to experience some of the aftermath at first hand.*]

A week later, William marched slowly along the south coast, devastating as he went. He took Sandwich, the chief naval port, to secure the harbour needed for reinforcements and supplies, and then captured Dover, which he burned. After Canterbury, he diverted to Winchester and then reached Southwark which he also burned before deciding the Thames bridge was too onerous to charge. Instead, William took a wide circle around London via Surrey, northern Hampshire and Berkshire cutting it off from its hinterland and its food supply. The great city capitulated after a slaughter of defiant young men and citizens in its central square.

Not so Winchester, the site of the treasury, which surrendered in November without a fight. Small columns of Norman soldiery, despatched from recently-arrived reinforcements from Southampton, travelled up the Itchen and held the city in a pincer with the main body at Basingstoke. The army was forced to march divided with a common *rendezvous* in order to survive: no village was capable of provisioning the whole force. At the instigation of the old king Edward's widow, queen Edith, who had lost four brothers in the year's battles, and backed by the Norman-supporting Old Minster, the townspeople of the capital of Wessex sent gifts and promises of submission. Guy, bishop of Amiens, said disparagingly that its citizens flocked to submit like 'flies to a running sore'.

One part of the organisation of the invasion that Odo made sure rested in his hands was the gathering of loot. His ships were allocated along the south English coast ready for the delivery of plundered goods. Treasures were sent to

Normandy in a daily stream. After unloading, adventurers and nobles scuffled at the small harbours demanding carriage to England to join the despoilation.

Following Odo's detailed instructions, here was my special job. Spaces on the returning ships were sold to the highest bidders by my team of harbour masters. Much of the gold, silver, jewellery, weapons, relics and ornaments was transferred to Bayeux to be listed by a battery of clerks under my supervision. Three English clerks, under offer of their lives, were sent to me by Odo to provide English names, values and importance of unknown items. I quickly acquired a working knowledge of Anglo-Saxon. Gifts were made through me to hundreds of churches in Normandy, France and Rome. Careful notes of these destinations were kept so that favours given could be reclaimed later. And, of course, an impressive selection was secreted away to adorn religious houses in Odo's episcopal see and, most importantly, the vast beckoning spaces of Bayeux's growing cathedral.

It was a hectic three months. We had barely the parchment to keep pace with the lists. My operation was kept afloat by returning Norman soldiers who had fought at Hastings and in the skirmishes on the roads to and around London. It was a twist of Christian logic that to kill or wound, even in battles approved by the pope, was a sin. Penance had to be done to win remission of the punishment which might be suffered in purgatory after death. The penitential of the papal legate, Ermenfrid, representative of pope Alexander, imposed lighter penances than normal of one year for those involved in this noble invasion but differentiated between those who killed before Hastings, at Hastings, and between Hastings and William's Christmas Day coronation. Those who plundered and ravaged must pray publicly and do good deeds for three years.

Odo, in his episcopal wisdom, halved these penances for those who guarded the sailings. I mused on the irony of it all. Successful soldiers worked for free in the ports of Normandy in the name of God in order to lessen their celestial penalties. Their task was to land goods stolen from English churches and monasteries and to deliver them to others in Normandy.

Near exhaustion, I was sought out by Adam. He and I were ordered to Canterbury where Odo was installed. We were, perhaps, both twenty-one.

2 A BLESSED LOOTING, 1067

Amidst all the pious claptrap about promised kingship, the main reason for the invasion was to loot England's wealth. After a few months of hard pillaging, my Lord Odo was established as the second most important man in England after the king. I already knew first hand, indeed I was a party to it, that he had no scruples about plundering English churches and abbeys to decorate his own institutions in Normandy. As I was quickly to discover, he showed great cunning in his double-dealing over English land. In truth, he was a ravening wolf, the evil genius of the conquest. I became increasingly scared of him and of my association with him.

I also found that I was scared of great seas as our boat heaved to the wave tops after leaving Rouen and the calm of the Seine. I did the best I could with *Thor* and the other horses while at the same time clinging to anything I could find. Adam spent most of the voyage revisiting his dinner of the previous evening. We, grandsons of Scandinavian raiders, did nothing to live up to our seafaring heritage.

As we disembarked at Sandwich, Odo's troops were clearly in charge of the port. Supplies were piled in general order and trains of carriage mules left frequently to supply the army. Long-haired Saxons provided much of the labour. Tension, even hatred, was evident with frequent muted insults which occasionally flared into scuffles. At Dover, men swarmed over the burgeoning castle walls which grew in strength even as we watched. They dominated the harbour where more jostling boats were crammed. Waves raced and crashed into the narrow space making the sea mad with foam.

Our party of ten was well-armed and horsed. We rode first the twelve miles to Canterbury, its houses still smouldering as a lesson for some petty resistance. At the cathedral, with its many empty niches, we received instructions to continue north east to Trenley Park. Odo was energetically enlarging the house and reinvigorating the old deer park with its rounded corners and external ditch. He explained to us, arms flapping with frustration, that the central ridge meant the land was liable to flooding where its poor quality sands and gravels ran down to sea marshes.

Odo was a worried man, his time torn between helping William to consolidate a shaky hold on the south of England, but all the while busy with acquiring personal land in all corners of that part of the kingdom that had submitted. His other guests were Hugh de Port, who was known to us, especially to Adam, and two of his knights, Vital and Wadard, who had both volunteered following my work at Neuilly. These men led Odo's squadrons at Hastings where Hugh killed many Englishmen from his horse in single combat.

Scarcely had refreshments been delivered than Odo expounded with brutal frankness about the precariousness of the invasion.

Hastings was a far from decisive battle: it did not result in immediate and complete submission. The Saxon earls Edwin and Morcar were not involved in Harold's defeat and now waited to see how the wind blew. A second army was expected from the Danish shires north of the Thames that had not yet seen a Norman soldier. The Norman command was staggered that London with its 25,000 people had not fought harder and that Winchester had succumbed without raising a finger while Exeter with, perhaps, 3,000 inhabitants resisted. At William's Christmas coronation in London, the acclamation had to be shouted twice, once in English and once in French. Worse, the Normans soldiers were so worried about the din that they started to fire the city believing there was a riot. 'There was a truce, but the English will never again trust us. They just wait to take revenge.'

Norman ships were perpetually at sea expecting the English fleet to blockade our toehold army, Odo continued. Kings Malcolm in Scotland and Swein of Denmark were expected to make common cause in the midst of the disorder to reclaim the land of Cnut. If the English could only agree on an alternative king, it would give them unity of purpose and a determination to resist.

'We control the towns, but not the countryside. Small bands of unconnected malcontents murder passing Normans and then melt into the woods. We likely have many years of bloody fighting ahead,' declared Odo. 'We need to have a careful plan and we need to be ruthless otherwise we can still be thrown back into the sea.

'If we are to lose we need to speed up the transfer to Normandy of English treasure so that there will be victory in defeat. At the moment, we need Anglo-Saxon expertise in government. If we are to win, we need to replace their control. Then, we need to replace their ownership of the land.'

Odo had been gazing over his marshy chase. He turned to face Adam and I for the first time.

'And that's where you two come in,' he said. The salt wind blew in from Normandy and I felt a drop in temperature as pockets of sweat formed under my jerkin. The English winter was gathering pace.

'At Hastings, two hundred of Harold's thegns fell with some 2,000 more of middle rank.[1] Some of their estates have already passed to our worthy barons in payment for their victory. We need to identify the estates of all these fallen traitors. We know that Harold's royal officials at Winchester hold lists of all estates and their possessors which indicate their tax liability.

'Some of this work has already begun, but it is haphazard. You, Gilbert, are to make this a tightly controlled investigation answerable only to me. I will take your work to our gracious king, my brother, for approval.'

My new job was to travel to Winchester, identify the fallen thegns, seize the tax lists and turn them into charters of distribution for the reward of our barons. I was excited at the opportunity to see the old capital and pleased that my work would be important and, if successful, deserving of recognition.

Odo took me slightly to one side, but within the hearing of Hugh. 'I expect, of course, that my own extensive involvement, and that of my lieutenants, will be properly recognised as befitting our contribution to the armada. This commitment led, of course, to your rise in my employment.'

All I could do was to nod with a slight bow of deference and acceptance.

'And you, dear Adam, will accompany Gilbert, our loyal servant, to Winchester and will introduce him there to your brother Eudo who serves as the king's steward. Eudo also understands my wishes. He will smooth Gilbert's path.'

Adam's reward was enticing. Hugh de Port currently held most of Kent for Odo. When all was underway at Winchester, Adam was to return to Dover as castellan, complete its fortifications, and guard England's south eastern approaches with a fleet.[2] All land around was to be at his command.

---

1 Thegn: Aristocratic retainers of senior Anglo-Saxon noblemen.
2 Castellan: A governor of a castle and its surrounding territory.

'That will free my dear Hugh,' announced Odo, 'to accompany me to Winchester where I have other work for him. I have granted Vital and Wadard estates near Dover and they will be ready to assist you, Adam.'

We stayed one night. As I lay in an uncomfortable cot in a room shared with three others who snored with decreasing rhythm, I mused how easy and how far it was possible to advance in the Norman world if morality was not an issue. Skills were respected and sought out regardless of birth right. After the king, Odo probably had the largest network of knights, clerks and secret men trained in Bayeux for this time and ready to do his bidding. But it was a dangerous world managed by avaricious and mercurial nobles and bishops. As fast as one could rise so could one fall. I resolved never to seek high office but to try, as far as I could, to work in the shadow of the aspiring great men. Perhaps, then, I would survive to old age.

Odo instructed us not to take the sea route to Southampton and Winchester, but to travel overland, news we both heard with joy, especially Adam, the putative admiral. In part, Odo said, the choice of the land route was because of fear of English raiders, but there was a more subtle reason.

'If you go via the port,' he said, 'news of your arrival in Winchester will precede you and harm could be done to your work. By land, you can slip into the city before anyone can do you foul.'

In the morning, winter arrived with a biting wind. Snow fell lightly causing concern that our path, although well-trod, might be lost. Not far from Canterbury, tracking on a ridge north above the river plain, we passed under a dense canopy of yew woods which all but excluded the pale daylight. The ground was black with needles that allowed nothing to grow. No birds called. The silence was palpable around the steady plod of hooves. Low branches were gripped by ice and I felt, for the first time, that I was in a foreign land. We spread out for fear of Saxon arrows and occasionally sensed, but did not see, small dark forms shift in the mist. It was a place of goblins, grotesque, malicious and greedy for gold.

At midday on the fourth day, we came to the source of the Wey and climbed through beech trees to the watershed and a hamlet called Medstead. A few bedraggled mud and plaster shacks stood around with their chickens and bare vegetable plots. Between the old fort and the small timber church, by a pond busy with ducks, there was a two-storey cottage built in part of thin Roman red brick. It was a *medehalla*, a tavern selling mead. Above the door, the head of a monster was rough carved. Inside, a young woman, the *meddere*, wrapped shapeless against the cold, served us each a small platter of unleavened flat bread smeared with honey and some mead warmed with a poker from the hearth. She exhibited as much ill grace as she could display without driving us away. One of Adam's men grabbed her by the waist and pulled her to his lap. Before he sensed his error, the poker was burning the back of his hand. Everyone was shouting. Two men rushed from the back room. Swords and knives were drawn.

It was my first direct experience of the tension that hovered raw in the countryside. Adam barked at his men and they flinched under his glare. I pulled the girl outside towards the pond and gave a half apology.

'You speak our language, Norman pig.'

'Not as well as I would like, but pigs are quick learners.'

Her face had come clear of her headcloths. She gave me a smile which turned my heart.

'I see you dropped your drink, pig. Shall I fill your trough?'

'Call me pig again and I shall hand you back to that knight who took such a fancy to you. I need my authority in front of the men as I am still a young porker. And, yes, please, fill my beaker and here are some coins to do the same for all the others. It will show them that there is no ill feeling left. Then the danger will pass.'

Her eyes were deep blue amongst long corn hair. We locked gaze for a few seconds. Then, she got up and did as I suggested. There were a few ribald comments, but she let them pass. As she poured my mead, I told her that my name was Gilbert and that I had come a few days ago from Bayeux in Normandy.

'Are you Odo's men,' she asked?

'We are Odo's men ... and the king's.'

'My name is Ailgifu,' she replied. 'I am the granddaughter of Ælfric, once ealdorman of Wessex.[3] His brothers were royal thegns. They had the loyalty of over one hundred ceorls, freemen. This is my cottage and this was Ælfric's land. We have fallen on difficult times. My brothers and I keep bees here and in nearby Ropley and I brew and sell the mead and honey – as you know.'

I asked about the monster above the door.

---

3   Ealdorman: The most prestigious local appointment of a West Saxon king who would lead in battle, preside over courts and levy taxation.

She explained it was a cockatrice, a two-legged dragon with a rooster's head that ate human flesh.

'We believed it came from a duck's egg incubated by a toad. It was laid in the crypt of Wherwell Priory near Andover which was founded by Ælfthryth, murderess of St Edward, as an act of penitence. My grandfather's family held the manor house next door for queen Elfrida and we used to play there. The cockatrice used to chase us around the grounds. Your 'monster' is my whim to remind me of happier times when we were a free country.'

I pondered the story while wondering what other nest I had stumbled into when Ailgifu interrupted my thoughts.

'Perhaps, being new to our country, you have not heard of my grandfather? He was one of the most trusted men of king Æthelred. He was killed fighting for Edmund Ironside against Cnut and the Danes at Assandun. That was fifty years ago, the last time we were invaded before your usurper pig William came.'

I cautioned her. 'Some of the men in there would kill you now for what you have just said. I understand the anger, but what use is it if you are dead. And who would look after the bees?'

She softened. 'You are right, of course, but then so am I.'

Who knows when that moment comes, the one the poets write about? It was unexpected, unwished even. Was it beauty, character, independence? Was I already lonely in a strange country?

I swung into *Thor*'s saddle. Ailgifu stroked his muzzle. 'We had horses once.'

'When I pass this way next, I would like another drink of your mead,' I offered. 'It is good.'

'Oink,' she said, but she smiled.

As I trotted off, Adam spurred his horse alongside.

'You need to be careful who you upset. It would be no contest if it came to a sword fight with one of my men. I would have to bury your body in the forest and blame the Saxons.'

'I'll explain that I acted to protect the mead seller only to obey my Lord Bishop's stricture to approach Winchester without fuss.'

'Do not be too clever,' he cautioned. 'I'll make it right'. He dropped back to the man with the wounded pride and scalded hand.

After a couple of hours, following mostly the verges of the old Roman road, now in rutted disrepair, we paused on the slopes of St Giles Hill to take our first view of Winchester. After crossing a ford in the late afternoon, we slipped into the city via the Durngate without challenge from the casual sentries. The immediate market square was empty, but the wide Alwarne and High streets were lively with the noise of busy craftsmen: coin minters, gold and silversmiths, soap makers and hosiers. We caused little notice among the well-fed families intent on making money from the needs of their Norman conquerors. A single walled enclosure separated the royal palace of the Wessex kings and their three minsters from the tumult of the city. A Conqueror's Hall was under construction, piles of building material all around. I was awed and so was Adam who echoed my thoughts, 'I have not travelled as much as I would have liked, but I have heard that this place compares favourably with any in Europe north of the Alps.'

The king was absent hunting with a small party in his appropriated forest west of Southampton. Eudo Dapifer, William's newly appointed steward, ignored protocol and came quickly to the palace courtyard where he threw his arms around his smaller brother, lifting him off the ground. It seems our passage through Durngate had not gone unnoticed; our arrival was anticipated.

'Work starts tomorrow,' he said. 'I understand that you have an important task, Gilbert. Tonight, I have rooms while my Lord the king is away and a good meal prepared for you all. But first, a small present for you.'

Eudo signalled to a young man who stepped from the shadows.

'I thought you would need help from the beginning,' said Eudo. 'This is Lēofric who is a distant relative of Stigand, our much loved and much despised bishop of Winchester and Canterbury. Lēofric is an outstanding scholar from our New Minster, well thought of, speaks English and Latin and is advanced with his Norman. He was about to depart for an abbey to teach novices, but I have purloined him for you. He is yours to work with and direct during your time here.'

Lēofric had the fashionable long flaxen hair of the English, a little unkempt under an odd dark red hat. His face was flat, open and without pockmarks. We were the same height and build which is to say, ordinary. I decided he would benefit from a spare tunic. When he looked directly at me his eyes sparkled and I caught a glimpse of someone I thought I knew. [*Lēofric became a dear friend and we were to work together for thirty years. Later, he offered to share his birthday when he found that I did not have one.*]

The creative scholarship of the Anglo-Saxons was well recognised from its old well-spring, the Benedictine bishop Æthelwold who worked one hundred years before. His monasteries, and particularly the Winchester minsters, produced a great flow of original illustrated volumes, drawings and books in English and in Latin. They also translated and transcribed existing classics embracing musical composition, medicinal and herbal treaties, poems studded with Greek references and advanced arithmetical and astronomical texts. Æthelwold's intellect introduced rules of grammar and metre and exhorted a striving for great things. By the first half of the eleventh century, the Winchester standard was known and used in all parts of the country, far in advance of Norman, French or Germanic writings. Many of his pupils became abbots, bishops and even archbishops in England mirroring Odo's young charges from Bayeux in the Norman empire. I was, I quickly recognised, very lucky with my gift.

Over our meal, we agreed that Adam could leave as soon as he wished after he had explored this foreign city. He was anxious to take up his new position at Dover and everyone at table was conscious of not keeping Odo waiting, but also wary of his imminent arrival with Hugh de Port on an unknown mission.

I pressed Lēofric in private about Stigand's notoriety. He was renowned across Christian Europe for being Edward the Confessor's loyal man and a trusted advisor who had served six kings from Cnut to the current day. The core problem, however, was that Stigand held both the bishoprics of Winchester and Canterbury simultaneously. For this pluralism, he had been excommunicated by five successive popes.

'The old man cannot survive much longer even if he is also the royal treasurer,' said Lēofric. 'The whole of Rome seems against him. My Lord king has found it politic to have Stigand's support and advice just as he finds it helpful to have assistance from the remaining Saxon household officials and the sheriffs. However, I hear that William's patience is wearing thin. One of the least believable reasons for the invasion was the need to reform the English church. It stands accused of pluralism, concubinage, the buying and selling of ecclesiastical favours as well as tolerating worldly prelates. How different is Normandy, I wonder?

'William has asked pope Alexander to send legates to help him challenge the English clergy. Any reform must start with deposing Stigand.'

I thought that Odo represented all these Christian crimes. If Odo was drawn into any papal investigation, William's cause would be vulnerable and could become embarrassing.

'You are dangerously frank to a stranger and an enemy,' I suggested.

He shrugged. 'No enemy, I hope,' he replied, 'but I must go where the devil drives if I am to survive in this dangerous new world.'

I asked Lēofric whether it would be possible to meet Stigand.

'If I were you I would stay away. I see him only rarely. When things do start to go wrong it would be better not to be in the same room.'

Lēofric's advice seemed wise.

'By the way,' he added, 'would you like me to find some rooms in the town away from the palace at the expense of the royal writing office and library? As you will see, the palace has few, cramped cells and you might prefer the greater freedom offered outside the wall if your work takes some time. Accommodation is difficult and getting worse. The Conqueror ordered the destruction at Christmas of about fifty houses to make way for his castle. More houses are being pulled down outside the town walls to enlarge the ditch and improve the defensive view.'

So I came, within a few days, to have an upper floor apartment in a timber framed house with wooden shingles set back a few paces from the frontage of Scowrtenestret. It was one of a number held by the abbot whose principal interest lay in the New Minster school and whom I never met. Downstairs lived a quiet, aged clergyman and his wife who, by a back door, had easy access to St Michael's churchyard, his place of occasional work. Immediately around were Jewish goldsmiths and numbers of shoemakers. The North Gate was a stone's throw. It was, Lēofric assured me, one of the quieter streets because of these occupations and, besides, was only ten minutes' walk to the palace and its offices. [*It suited me so well that two years later when the clergyman died and his wife left for a widow's church charity and I had need of more space, I took the whole house.*]

The next morning in the New Minster writing office on the fourth floor of its tower, I explained my task to Lēofric. We had one of those circular discussions about the morality of him abetting the ejection of the families of Saxon thegns from their land, some of them perhaps distant blood kin. In contrast, I offered the reality of the invasion, the inevitability of what was to happen and his own personal security when Eudo heard that Lēofric had declined his instruction. I admit I thought my new servant had the more attractive argument so I offered a small compromise. Working as a team, we would be alert to injustice. We would seek ways to mitigate its worst effects by acting safely in the background.

We shook hands and set to work.

A table had been set aside for us in the main library which was staffed by two elderly monks, eyes too diminished to continue their craft of illustrating manuscripts. Both were well known to Lēofric as were most of the other clerks as well as those in the Treasury where the new broom had not yet reached. We decided first to start our list of slain thegns with what we knew. I gave out that it was a question of honouring the dead, a complete deceit. This was helped because we assumed, rightly as it turned out, that Harold's defeated army was officered overwhelmingly by men from the southern and eastern parts of England. Men were despatched to the Saxon towns to ascertain who had died. Inaccurate answers, it was pointed out, would invite further interest by the king's tax collectors. As I laboured over these lengthening manuscripts, Lēofric checked the names against the hidage lists that were held in Winchester for the burhs created by King Alfred the Great for the defence of the kingdom of Wessex.[4]

In the previous century, after his victories over the Danes at Edington and Fulham, Alfred built the burhs, a large number of new forts, to add to the old fortified towns. These strongpoints extended as far as Exeter in the west and Warwick and Worcester in the north. Stone walls were repaired and perimeter ditches deepened. In case of raids, the towns provided a place of refuge for the rural population who lived nearby. They led in time to the creation of a unified kingdom.

Local taxation to fund the fortifications was based on the food required from each area. This was called the hide which varied in its acreage, generally settling at 120. Winchester was by far the most prominent and was reckoned at 2,400 hides while its port at Southampton represented but 150. Over time, each hide not only specified the food rent, but also the other common tax burdens of military service, fortress work and bridge repair. Beneficial reductions to favoured landowners were also noted.

By the end of the second week, William, our king, returned to Winchester. The pace of work seemed to double; the tension in the town was palpable. Lēofric and

---

4   Hidage: A tax or tribute paid to the royal exchequer for every hide of land.

I recognised that some landholders had anticipated their vulnerability through the burghal hidage. Some of the calfskins were missing, others crudely torn. I suspected Lēofric and asked him if he had broken his vow. This led immediately to our first row, two days of sullenness and then reconciliation. Questioning the two old monks produced fearful silences. We decided to hold our peace and, in line with our pact, not to do unnecessary harm.

Odo and Hugh de Port arrived in Winchester to great ceremony. Unlike Eudo's greeting of Adam, William waited in the throne room in regal splendour for the necessary obeisance of his brother. Formalities over, the ensuing parties were described as 'enthusiastic', 'unseemly' and 'unchristian'.

William left in March for Normandy where he stayed for most of the rest of the year. He took with him the Englishmen who worried him most: archbishop Stigand; one of the Saxon claimants to the throne, Edgar the Ætheling; and the earls of Mercia and Northumberland, the brothers Edwin and Morcar. Two regents were left to rule England in his absence: Odo, of course, now earl of Kent, and William FitzOsbern, previously William's guardian and the best officer in the army, who was granted extensive lands and given the title earl of Hereford. Hugh de Port was appointed sheriff of Hampshire in recognition of his feat of arms.

Hugh came with Odo to our library table to understand our progress. I showed the list of thegns known to have fallen or been exiled, which already stood at just over one thousand, and the location of their major estates and in what region. The next stage, starting immediately, was to investigate the exact hidage through oral testimony at local courts. It would be an easy matter for the royal representatives of the sheriff or perhaps special commissioners to demand the information.

Odo did not hesitate, but pledged thirty knights to our direction. Their visits to the corners of conquered England were accompanied by writs, formal instructions in English and authenticated by an impression of the king's seal hanging from one corner. Producing these meant the employment of five clerks.

Once estate identification was complete, distribution of the sequestered land became a question of power and politics. With Odo and Hugh in town, it was more a matter of them choosing the choicest sweetmeats from the plate and cementing the disbursements before the king's return.

I felt that Lēofric and I had lived up to our mutual promise. Certain dead thegns, some small estates, including the hamlet called Medstead and some fields in Ropley, did not appear in the lists or, if they did, carried false information. We had done the best we could and it strengthened our relationship.

The day following Odo's visit, an unsigned letter was delivered from Hugh de Port. It contained a simple list of about fifty manors in Hampshire including, I noticed, with an eye to peaceable relations with Medstead, the manors at Chawton, Dummer, Herriard, Preston and Brown Candover and [*significantly for Odo a few years ahead*] Portsmouth and the Isle of Wight. Our work was the way in which Hugh de Port became eventually one of the principal landlords of the south and how the extent of Odo's own lands continued him second only to the king. The manor at Chawton was to be used to fund Oda, Hugh's native dapifer.[5]

The wholesale expropriation of land was deeply resented by the heirs and kin of the deceased or exiled thegns who expected to inherit estates. Instead, only tiny plots were left for widows and orphans. The 180 Norman barons who replaced them quickly became the dominant aristocracy, fulfilling the beginning of the plan for the complete mastery of England. They prided themselves on being a race part, defined by their special characteristics: illustrious ancestors, legal status, functions, wealth, style of life, prowess at hunting and always, of course, their land. Their world was divided into three groups, all required to support the king: those who fought, those who prayed, and those who worked.

Resentment brought a spirit of dogged resistance though many preferred surrender to starvation. The offence was compounded when the new Norman lords sought to marry the heiresses, widows and daughters of the deceased thegns. Willingly marrying a Norman was considered by many Englishmen to be consorting with the enemy. Many women in fear of forced marriages entered convents and became nuns.

One evening, comfortable with glasses and a bottle, Lēofric went into his room and returned with a chequered board. He placed it on a stool between us.

'I think that it is time that we sharpened your mind, Norman,' he said.

And, so, I was introduced to the game of chess. Lēofric poured the pieces from a black cloth bag tied with a gaudy drawstring and slowly explained their

---

5   Dapifer: A steward appointed by the legal ruling monarch to represent them in a country.

purpose. The idea of a game of intellect between two players with nothing left to chance, the roll of a dice or the turn of a card, had never occurred to me. I loved the solid pieces carved with skill from boar tusk. Even more, I loved the way they mirrored the world outside our door: the king with his queen and his castles, bishops that never moved in a direct line, knights that used their rapid horses to skirt the enemy and to attack from an unexpected direction, and, of course, the foot soldiers that would be sacrificed for the royal good.

Lēofric was a good player and a patient teacher. We tried our hand almost every night claiming Hampshire manors as our prize. As my understanding grew, I realised that my opponent preferred dash to strategy. Our moves reflected our personalities. While Lēofric sought to overwhelm with surprise and force, I was happy to wait, quietly dodging and probing, seeking misplaced confidence and the mistake that would follow.

After two months, I paid an afternoon visit to Medstead taking Lēofric with me and escorted by two men-at-arms. It was a dangerous time to travel even close to Winchester. Small groups of our men were regularly attacked, especially as they passed along wooded tracks. From the start, the new local lords made use of existing English and Danish encampments, former Roman fortifications and even older forts many of which were mere ring works. The hill of beech trees by Medstead became such a notorious spot so that even the very run down fortification near the village pond was pressed into service. Local men were required to do manual repairs and then guard the flimsy walls with four men to every pole whenever trouble was anticipated.

A resistance movement, which we called *silvatici*, gradually established bases in remote areas of forest and marsh such at the North Yorkshire hills and the fens of East Anglia and sometimes deep into the shires around London and Winchester. After a sudden flight of arrows, the 'wildmen' disappeared leaving pain, deep frustration and death. Reprisal against, possibly, innocent nearby villagers was swift and thoughtless. Our soldiers' morale suffered in the midst of desertions and constants skirmishes. Desperate Norman wives begged husbands to return home even to the extent of threatening adultery. William's response was to promise more lands and revenues for those who built his dream.

Ailgifu's welcome was one of anger at all things Norman. She came to the door of her cottage and then stood before me as I dismounted. I introduced Lēofric, but she hardly acknowledged him. Her disgust overflowed.

'Such brutal slaughter cannot go unpunished,' she announced. 'The innocent and the guilty are condemned alike to die by slow starvation. Helpless children, young men in the prime of life and hoary grey-beards are perishing of hunger.'

My hopes of furthering our relationship fell like ice rain.

'The almighty judge watches over high and low alike and he will weigh the deeds of all men in a fair balance and as a just avenger will punish wrong-doing,' she continued.

I stood head down as if all the fault of the invasion were on my shoulders.

'I hoped for a warm welcome and to share some mead with you …,' I began, but she cut me off.

'Your soldiers march and ride through here on their way to and fro between London and Winchester. They take our scarce water for their horses without a care. It is a wonder we have any food left and if there will be any woman undefiled.'

'I will try to speak to those close to the king and to tell him what …'

'We have a long-standing tradition in England which is opposed to having bastard kings,' she whipped back. 'Kings are only legitimate if they are chosen by the bishops and elders of the people and not resulting from adulterous or incestuous procreation. Your William has stolen the throne over the dead bodies of Anglo-Saxon thegns, my people.'

To my surprise, Lēofric intervened. 'It is what we were talking about, master,' he said. 'It is why the claim has to be made that William is king by hereditary right and by the grant of God. It is why he was anointed with holy oil and cultivates holy men. The latest official argument, my Lord, as you know, is that Harold was a usurper and was never king. It is why, when the papal legates come, their approval is so necessary.'

Ailgifu stared at him.

'Today there are two Englands,' she retorted. ' One is free and the other part is occupied, governed directly by your Odo and the other Norman lords. It is only managed with the help of collaborators. There are half a dozen men with greater claim to the throne than some supposed arrangement made in a gaol in Normandy. Now, I hear there is to be great ceremony in Westminster when the king returns with his wife and cousin, a marriage refused by the pope as unlawful by close blood. She is to be crowned our queen. It is shameful.'

I thanked heaven that we were speaking in English and could not be understood by our escort. I remounted and looked down at her where she shook with rage.

'I had some good news for you about your village,' I said. 'I had hoped to share it with you in friendship. I shall come back here once more to try for a last time. Think on that. I wish you well.'

I wheeled and left at pace and was near the source of the river Itchen in the valley below before Lēofric and the others caught up. We rode in silence until we reached an inn on the outskirts of a small village where we stopped for refreshments.

'You know,' said Lēofric, 'I think she likes you a lot.'

It was my turn to stare at him.

'No one who hates your people that much would waste their time lambasting someone they did not care about. You could be a lucky man.'

Back in Winchester, I sought out Hugh. I explained the importance of the pass of Alton to the good communications between the two capitals. I told him that I had cause to visit the local villages, like Chawton, Farringdon, Medstead and Ropley, and the reinvigorated fort, as part of my work. The local people were peaceable in my opinion, but were being sorely tried by brutish behaviour from our soldiery. The king passed through the area regularly. A softer hand might keep the area quiet. As Hugh's land was involved, the last thing we wanted as we distributed further manors, was for his authority to be questioned.

I thought I had gone too far. Hugh looked at me as he turned matters over. Then he took my hand and thanked me for my good advice.

Lēofric sat down sharply on a stool.

'Love has made you mad to take such risks,' he said.

3 EDITH AND HER MARZIPAN, 1068

While the king was on his tour of triumph in Normandy, the situation in England deteriorated rapidly. The two regents, FitzOsbern and Odo, swollen with pride, ignored what seemed to me the reasonable pleas of the English for impartial judgements. There were many stories of support for men-at-arms when they were guilty of plunder and rape. Complainants and their families often paid with their lives. There was an arrogance and a disregard that belied the frequent claims of even-handedness.

Lēofric acted as a conduit for the mood of the people. He could get impassioned.

'The English groan aloud for their lost liberty,' he assured me. 'They plot ceaselessly to find some way of shaking off the intolerable and unaccustomed yoke!' Despite the seriousness of the general situation, I couldn't resist a smile at his language.

We laboured away, making the situation worse by identifying and listing forfeited estates and their new landlords. Eminent barons or their stewards were frequent visitors, some abusive, some wheedling, almost all offering bribes in attempts to consolidate their lands instead of receiving piecemeal allocations.

I spent much time deflecting complaints and decisions to Odo whose dithering was a constant surprise to me. I heard his counter arguments often. As king, William owned all land in his realm. Its distribution to reward rank and service was only for as long as the monarch saw fit. His seal was required on all charters. In practice, once a decision was made, it would take a gross misdemeanour or a risk of a baronial revolution to take any manors back. Every two days, if required, a royal messenger left Winchester for Normandy with a pouch full of documents. Within a week, they were returned with approvals and comments written by William's travelling clerks for the king could not read or write complex documents. After some months, William's deviousness became apparent. The distribution of scattered manors was designed to ensure that any vassal's power base could not be easily organised to rise up in revolt as one.

I left my next trip to Ailgifu for a month hoping to cause her concern that she had lost my interest.

'You have returned, my Lord Gilbert,' she welcomed. 'I thought you might need more time for your anger to subside.'

'I am no lord, my Lady, but a clerk and advisor to bishop Odo, earl of Kent. I am keen to try your mead again.'

'Then you shall have some. The sun is warm. Come, sit with me in the shade.'

She told me the king had passed by Medstead on the feast of Pentecost. He was taking Matilda of Flanders to Westminster to be crowned his queen.

'Your queen as well, now,' I suggested. Ailgifu spat into the dirt.

'The marriage is damned by the pope,' she retorted. 'We have a bastard king and his wife, despite all her royal blood, is his cousin.' She paused, then, 'I expected to see you pass by as one of the guests.'

I couldn't tell whether she was joking or disappointed.

I explained that I was too lowly born and had not even seen the king let alone be invited to his wedding. It was time to tell her of my arrangements with the allocations of her ancestral lands in Medstead and Ropley. She said she was grateful and I believed she was genuine, but then became thoughtful.

'I assume that this is just putting off the evil day?' she suggested. 'Last week, I had church stewards and their Norman lords from Alresford come round to collect our silver pennies and too much hard-grown produce from our tenants, all to pay for their fine costumes and fat bellies. They move freely on horseback from place to place displaying their superiority and enjoying the hunting as they go.'

'Who can say,' I replied. 'Who can say. There is a twisted road through this mad world and I do not believe that anyone knows where it leads.'

And so it went for several months through the summer. I would choose days and times of day to visit when I thought she was likely to be less busy. I was increasingly welcomed, but the greeting was always met with verbal sparring. Deference to a man, especially a Norman, was not part of Ailgifu's character. I came to respect her the more, but the constant friction showed the ever-present discrepancies between our cultures. Each visit found some new cause for disagreement. She was often well versed in any gossip or legislation as it affected her hamlet and her people through frequent conversation with the many travellers who passed by. Her knowledge of the Norman language had improved considerably. I learned that far from occupying an area of quiet, the English in Medstead were like dry kindling and waited only for a spark.

That third visit, I travelled alone. Ailgifu sat beside me as I was served by an old man.

'Perhaps I can guess the good news that you spoke of at the end of your last visit. Oda's steward rode up from Chawton and said I was to let him know if there was any unpleasantness from passing soldiery. It was the first time I had met him. Then, the next day the serjeant from the fort walked over, took a drink and said he was here for my protection. I'm very impressed by your influence. Thank you, Lord Gilbert.'

She waved for a refill for me from the servant. His clothes were more rough than normal so I asked his status.

'He is a slave,' she replied. 'All the villages around here have half a dozen slaves or more. It has always been that way.'

'But, I didn't know you had slaves. I've never noticed any.'

'Well, you wouldn't,' she said. 'They are slaves. Do you have a problem? Aren't you Normans trying to make slaves of my people?'

I admitted to being shocked, especially in this sleepy hamlet. Normans to my knowledge didn't keep slaves although the conditions of the many estate servants did not suggest much freedom. But, then, if you killed unarmed people during invasions and reprisals, took hostages, mutilated captives, locked individuals away for years on end, what was the difference at the end of the day?

I had met one of the few Normans who had been to Bristol. He told me that he had sighed over rows of wretches bound together with ropes. 'They were young people of both sexes whose beautiful appearance and youthful innocence might move barbarians to pity,' he said. Each day, they were exposed to prostitution and offered for sale. Slavery was big business in Bristol. No part of the coast in the west was safe from marauders.

'I think it is the simple idea of buying and selling people,' I mused to Ailgifu, 'especially when they are bought by the pagans in Dublin, Waterford and Wexford and taken to the infidels in Spain and North Africa for harems and the militias. Are we not all equal before God in heaven?'

I paused. 'Where did your slaves comes from?'

'They came from my grandfather's time during the wars against the Danes, but we have a couple of Celts as well. The Norsemen also enslaved many of our people. I hear the Scots under king Malcolm still raid for slaves in the north.'

'You mean your slaves are not the people who were first captured, but their children?'

'Great grandchildren, more like. We call them *æhts*. They can not go anywhere; they are our property. Most of them wouldn't move now even if they could. They wouldn't know where to go. Our men slaves plough the fields and dig the wells and bring up water. When the females are used by local men, their children are slaves also, if the man wishes it.'

It was the casualness of the discussion that disconcerted me most. To Ailgifu, owning a person was the most natural thing. In my turn, I felt sick inside.

'Do any of your slaves try to escape?' I asked.

'Not recently,' she replied, 'but there are lots of stories about slaves trying to reach St Swithun's tomb outside the Old Minster. For instance, a girl was manacled hand and foot for some misdeed and was due to be beaten. She prayed to the saint and her leg irons fell off. She ran all night to the grave in Winchester. Her master found her the next day and she was freed.'

'Have you ever freed any slaves?'

'Two. They were man and wife. I took them to the crossroads in the centre of the village where everyone can see what is happening. It is the place we use because the freed slaves are then able to go in any direction. But, they didn't; they stayed here. Alfrik and Fritha live behind the church where Alfrik's family has always lived.'

I needed time to think and felt it best to change the subject before I said something challenging and tempers flared. I suggested that on my next visit I brought a spare horse and she could show me the local countryside. She brightened considerably at the idea.

'I would love to ride again in the beech trees and along the ridge.'

Lēofric was waiting for me outside my house, dozing in the late afternoon sun, gently rocking on two legs of his stool. He raised one eyelid as I dismounted. Our work in the library was all but done and we both had agreeable time on our hands. One decision we had made was to spend a half-day or two each week in the library reading and researching our own interests.

I handed him the reins. Another of Lēofric's tasks was the care of *Thor*. What was Lēofric, I wondered: servant, slave or friend?

'How did it go?' he asked. 'Well enough? Have you fallen out again?'

I made to kick his seat away from underneath him, but he stood up quickly pretending to use his stool to protect himself against unfair attack.

'Be careful, I have important news which may change your life.'

'All right, play your game. What is it you have for me?'

'Well, it is summed up in this humble stool. You know, of course, that 'stōl' (he lengthened the vowel sound to make his point) is the Northmen's word for a seat. That is the word we have used here since the time of Cnut. Now you bastard French have arrived and bring with you your 'chaise'. Where will this all end? The invasion extends to where we put our bottoms. What if some bloodthirsty tribe of Danes invades again, then will we all be back to 'stōl'?'

'Enough, enough, Lēofric. Will you get to the point before I have you skewered?' He loved that kind of wordplay.

'The point, Lord, is that your gracious sheriff, Hugh de Port, seeming custodian of most of this part of Wessex, wishes to see you as soon as you return. He has a new task for you from Odo, our bishop, which will test your mettle. As your lowly servant, I am not party to the subject.'

He paused. 'But then, according to one of the maids in Hugh's chambers, you are to move to be near the nunnery at Wilton Abbey to act as an official messenger between Odo and Edith, the gracious queen, wife of the saintly Edward the Confessor. As you may not know, she is half Danish, very clever, good at languages and, say it softly, possibly a murderess, a not uncommon happening in a Saxon court.

'Hence, my suggestion, that you quickly get to know your *stōl* from your *chaise*.'

I grabbed the stool and sat on it, head in hands, wondering what on earth I had done to deserve this new assignment. I had never seen a queen before, let alone a crowned and dangerous one.

Hugh de Port was circumspect and friendly. He had reason to be grateful for the manors at Chawton and elsewhere.

'This is not an onerous duty, Gilbert,' he explained, 'but it does need tact. My lord Odo wants to know what the queen intends to do before anything bad becomes public. You are offered as her messenger. If she chooses not to use you at any time then we will know that something untoward is happening.' He passed over a letter of introduction.

'These are exalted circles for me,' I argued. 'I know none of the royal family nor the queen's courtiers. I would not want to offend through lack of schooling.'

'Take your servant Lēofric with you. He will be sensitive to much of the nuance for he has danced at the edges of these people. It is a test set by bishop Odo for you and for him, but it is more than that.'

Hugh gave me a rudimentary briefing which, thankfully, was added to later by Lēofric.

Queen Edith was one of nine children of the all-powerful Godwin family; her mother was the sister of a Danish earl who was Cnut's brother-in-law. She married king Edward when she was twenty and he double her age. The marriage lasted twenty years including a period when Edith was sent to a nunnery for a failure, so that gossip went, to produce any children.

Edith was a tough politician well versed in the nasty side of court politics. A few years ago, it was alleged at court that she acted for her brother Tostig and engineered the death of his rival, Gospatrick, the noble Northumbrian thegn.

What interested all the Norman elite, especially Odo, was how and if she would use her power. She was in the centre of the whirlpool that could upset the consolidation of the invasion.

'Consider the strings she is able to pull,' said Hugh. 'She is an anointed queen, half-Danish, one of the richest people in all England. Her husband was half-Norman. Indeed, he invited his Norman friends to his court in shoals. Edith was like a daughter to the old man and was present at his death supposedly warming his feet in her lap. Together with her brother, Harold, the usurper king, and the excommunicated bishop Stigand, she heard Edward's last words which may have been about the succession. She is the last surviving member of the Godwin family living in the country. She knows all the traitorous claimants to the throne and each of them would be delighted to have her support.

'And she has just commissioned a manuscript about her blasted family and her devious late husband. She has sent copies to everyone. She must have kept her scribes from bed for months.

'Find out what she is up to, but in no event upset her. Take as long as it needs.'

Lēofric and I decided to start by reviewing queen Edith's new manuscript, grandly called *Vita Ædwardi Regis qui apud Westmonasterium Requiescit*, 'The Life of King Edward who Rests at Westminster'. As the sun rose next morning, it was lying ready on our table having been rescued from the bishop's palace. There were fifty-one sheets written by an anonymous hand. However, the last page was written by Edith to Goscelin, who lived as secretary to bishop Herman in his nearby household at Ramsbury in Wiltshire. Edith thanked him for the 'faithful completion of his commission'. Goscelin of Saint-Bertin by St Omer, a Flemish Benedictine monk, was also chaplain to the nuns at Wilton Abbey, Edith's home. We did not know him.

When Lēofric laid down the final sheet, I pushed back on my bench.

'Well, what do you think?'

'I think that it is all about motive,' he said. 'First, what our gracious lady wishes to achieve and, second, what Odo and William want out of it which is probably never exactly the same thing.'

I said I thought her intent was clear enough. If things went badly, she could lose her money and her lands. She wouldn't want to fall foul of William. Her information to Goscelin for his inclusion was basically factual. She had reported her husband's dying instructions about the succession with sufficient ambiguity so that William and Harold's remaining supporters could argue in different directions. And, she had cleverly added layers to her own protection.

I flicked through the pile and came up with a sheet. 'Here's what she claimed the king said.'

> *May God be gracious to this my wife for the zealous solicitude of her service. For she has served me devotedly, and has always stood close by my side like a beloved daughter. And so from the forgiving God may she obtain the reward of eternal happiness.*

'Edward then reaches out to Harold.'

> *I commend this woman and all the kingdom to your protection. Serve and honour her with faithful obedience as your lady and sister, which she is, and do not despoil her, as long as she lives, of any due honour got from me.*

'It all depends,' said Lēofric, 'what you want *kingdom to your protection* to mean.'

'She also allows an undermining of bishop Stigand,' I added. 'He was the third big beast present at the death. What did Goscelin say?'

We too see God angered against the people on account of our deserving iniquities, and from us no penance or confession goes … That man Stigand will repent too late or not at all who thought that the blessed king … rambled owing to age and disease.

'That's him put in his place.'

'She is in her forties,' mused Lēofric. 'In that one year she lost her husband and then four brothers at Stamford and Hastings, all held to be in rebellion. Her country was invaded. She wants the reputation of her family to be reinstated both for her own and her history's sake. She would be most unsettled, raw even. By all accounts, she was, still is, a tough lady who likes to be thought well of.' He reached for another sheet.

'See, she has approved praise for her own liberal education, her piety, her talent for literature, languages and embroidery, and her physical beauty. Somewhere else, yes, here, Goscelin says that the queen was *self-effacing in public*, but a *pillar of strength behind the scenes; especially strong in counsel*. I think we know what is barely hinted at. She is not to be crossed. She has connections and can still bite.'

I suggested a cool drink while we discussed William's motives, quietly. Outside, I found one of the writing room servants idling and gave him money to bring a cold jug and cups down to the trees and shade at the river's edge. Passing through the King's Gate, the noise of industry and construction was muffled by the palace building. Downstream across the water two horse barges, freshly pulled from Southampton, were unloading. We settled on the grass, thinking to ourselves, until the boy came bustling up.

'I believe William had made an early understanding with Edith,' began Lēofric. 'Just two months after he invades, William comes to Winchester where the Treasury is intact. Winchester was Edith's town. Nobody puts up a fight. In fact, our noble king is welcomed by the brave burgers. Edith is then left to her own devices. She keeps her wealth and her lands and she also keeps her mouth closed.'

'Do not forget,' I interjected. 'Exeter is also loyal to Edith. In the rebellion two years ago, the local people supported the remnants of the Godwin family and refused to pay William's new taxes. A hostage was blinded in plain sight of the defenders. The siege lasted eighteen days despite tunnels under the walls. No one was punished after the women of the city paraded in surrender. I do not see him being that lenient again.'

Lēofric coughed quietly and looked around. He dropped his voice.

'It's plain enough,' he said. 'William calls Edward his kinsman and claims to rule over the country by hereditary right. He says that Edward promised him the kingdom, but no one in England knows of this. Edith's ambiguity at the death bed is vital. She has not claimed a role as regent or arbiter. The right answer is anyone's guess and any answer implies that someone is a liar. The more William explains the invasion by claiming to be the rightful heir of Edward, the more his respect for Edith, Edward's wife, must be evident. To do otherwise would undermine his position and might unleash the Saxons, the French, the Danes and even the Scots.

'And, no doubt, our Lord Odo will take a very close interest in what you report. He will have his own agenda.'

'So,' I summarised, 'my job at Wilton is to protect Edith from herself, if she will let me. If she is weakened, William is weakened.'

'Perhaps, we should have a boat standing by,' suggested Lēofric.

Before we set out, I made my delayed next visit to Medstead. There were increased attacks on solitary Norman travellers so I took Lēofric and two men-at-arms who were pleased to get away from their barracks and the ordered bustle. For the first time, Ailgifu showed open pleasure and walked quickly to embrace me.

'I see you have kept your promise and brought me a horse to ride,' she said, walking round the animal and nuzzling him. 'What is his name?'

I looked puzzled and glanced to Lēofric who shrugged.

'Ah,' said Ailgifu, 'no name? I shall call him, let me see, Gilbert, for he will know how to behave and to do what he is told.'

She was clearly a competent rider if a little rusty. She led off with my entourage following at a discreet distance. There were bees in the warm air called by the scent of afternoon clover. Stopping by a stone wall, she said that the hives were the other side, but it would be better to leave while the insects were at work. They could get angry at this time if disturbed.

'Our bees down in Ropley feed on borage which gives the honey a stronger taste,' she said.

Ailgifu pointed at some striking purple pink flowers.

'These are foxgloves. Around here we call them the flower of the fairies or fairy weed. See, they are shaped like the fingers of a glove. They bow down their heads when a fairy passes.'

We moved slowly through open bracken and grasslands, good only for the rough pasture of cattle and pigs. Ahead, on the ridge line, began the great wood of beech trees that stretched to Alton and Chawton. I felt at peace. It may seem strange considering all the travelling I had already done in this new country, but almost always I had followed well-used roads through districts which had a distinct character. Here, for the first time, I was picking my way along animal tracks and through small gaps in the vegetation. There was little cover for armed men.

Ailgifu met the drovers' track which came along the south side of the highest ground in the wet season and was evidently recently used by the amount of cattle dung and attendant flies. We crossed the London road which I knew well. Sharply carved boundary stones marked the unseen limits of Chawton and Farringdon. We wandered past regular shallow chalk pits and well-tended artificial rain-water ponds for there were no streams. Wattle hurdles lay in occasional piles where patches had been cropped and the stock was free to roam. Among these fences, permanent gates and stiles controlled pathways, especially those which led to the ponds or to occasional ploughlands. Later, I remembered some of the place names that Ailgifu called out: *Mint Mere*, *Feld Dene*, *Grenmeres Stigele*, the stile of the green pond; *Lammeres Geate*, the gate by the clay pond; *Bocmeres Stigele*, the gate to the stile at the pond of the beech trees; *Beanmeres Gate* at the pond where vetches grow; and *Hammerdean Gate* with its black hellebore.

At *Ravenscombe Gate* we rested to take in the view and had our customary disagreement, although perhaps less of an outright row this time. Ailgifu offered that for all the ground she knew, she had never been to Winchester, now the home of the Norman devils. She then asked with a smile why my men followed us when she was here to protect me.

'There is more bad news coming for you,' I said. 'So many Normans are turning up dead in suspicious circumstances in lonely places that I hear king William has decided to reimpose Cnut's hue and cry and the murdrum fine. William now sees Englishmen as having fickle minds who have turned away from loyalty by sinful conspiracy. Throughout the country, bandits are slaying soldiers whom the king has left behind to defend his kingdom.'

Ailgifu put her head in her hands and sighed deeply.

I pushed on. 'Murders are quite frequent. The law-abiding members of all communities are to be made responsible for curtailing their wilder spirits … like your brothers …'

It was crass and she exploded as I should have anticipated.

'So, all men are to suffer for the actions of the few. This is just another plot to steal our land by impoverishing us. Tell me how bad it is going to be.'

I argued the practice was time honoured, but admitted it was morally unpleasant.

'The plan is to stop assassinations by placing a heavy financial burden on each community,' I told her. 'What I have done, at some risk, is to copy the writ which is being prepared. I have done it so that you can be prepared … and all your family will know the consequences. This is what William plans to promulgate.'

> *I desire that all men who I have brought with me or who have come after me shall enjoy the benefit of my protection. And if one of them is slain, his lord shall arrest the slayer within five days if he can. If not, however, he shall begin a payment of forty-six marks of silver from the property of that lord as long as it lasts out. When however, the property of that lord fails, the whole hundred in which the murder is committed shall pay in common what remains.*

I decided to let her know it all.

> *All free men over the age of twelve years will be required to join a group of ten men, a tithing, led by a tithing man, so that they can defend themselves against a charge of wrong doing. Each of the members will be required to guarantee the good conduct of his fellow members. A whole village, like Medstead or Ropley, might go to make up a tithing. They will be obliged to produce in court any member of the tithing who was suspected of a crime and to raise a hue and cry if he flees. Any failure will result in a large fine.*

Ailgifu sat quiet for some minutes and then said, 'I think that we should go back now to my family's prison.' We didn't speak on the way home, the day ruined. When we arrived, there was no offer of mead, although the men-at-arms took some. Because I thought all was completely lost, I tried one last forlorn invitation, an attempt to blow a soft breeze on the embers of a dying relationship. I asked her if one day in a few weeks she would like to visit Winchester as my guest. To my great surprise, she accepted.

'You never know,' she said, 'when it might prove useful to have looked the devil in the eye.'

Lēofric prudently rode with the men-at-arms on our way home.

It was a gentle ride to the convent at Wilton Abbey, one of a pair of royally-connected nunneries serving Winchester, the other being at Amesbury. Wilton was the richest, most royal and most exclusive. It was enclosed with a wall, imposing, yet far from cut off from the world. The twenty-six nuns had a noble lifestyle and even had a collection of wild animals. Swein, king of Denmark, had destroyed the local town, but the abbey remained a regal favourite; Cnut and his queen, Emma, often visited. Edith was raised here and named after its patron saint. She had the wooden buildings remade in stone. Over time, some of the highest women in the land were housed either for protection or between marriages: King Edgar's daughter; Edward's aunt; Edith's mother, Wulfthryth; and Edgar's repudiated wife. The rooms were large enough to house important business meetings, for instance for major land transactions. Queen Edith was not the abbess, but there was no question who ruled the roost.

Comfortable lodgings had been arranged for us as towns were obliged to assist the king's messengers. Lēofric and I ate an early meal together which always caused raised eyebrows, but for what reason depended on your degree of Englishness. A servant was sent to the abbey with my letter of introduction and a request for an audience. We waited two full days for a reply; time passed nervously as we had explored the town within the first hour and sauntered down the hill to the gravel-bottomed River Wylye. The call when it came gave us thirty minutes' notice. Our strings were already being pulled and it didn't stop there. We arrived five minutes late and were told that meant a wait of another hour as another appointment had replaced us. It was all, of course, an act and Lēofric and I discussed being deliberately unimpressed when we finally gained entry.

However, all such thoughts disappeared when the door opened. Some people, not many, emanate power. Odo usually did [and William also when I finally saw him close to]. Others like Hugh de Port had power, but you did not sense it until you saw them in action with all their trappings. Edith was plainly dressed as a nun except for a large emerald ring on one hand, a renowned gift from her late husband. It was the only trace of royal finery, but it said everything: style, power, control and hard calculation. She was flanked by two noble ladies in matching black habits with expressionless faces. It was a tableau.

Edith was one of those women, I guessed, who became more beautiful as the years passed. I found myself wishing that Ailgifu could be there to see her queen. I wondered if I would be able to find the words to share the moment.

I bowed. Lēofric, a pace behind, was, I sensed, overawed, something I had never seen before. He genuflected as befitted a Saxon. I resisted reaching out to close his slack jaw.

'Your Highness,' I began, but I was cut across.

'Gilbert of Bayeux, you come most warmly recommended by your Lord, the bishop Odo.' Her head stayed still, but her eyes moved as she continued, 'as do you my fellow countryman, Lēofric. Do I know your families?'

Rank was established. Potential inclusion hinted. Room for manoeuvre limited. It was masterful.

'Sadly, no, Highness. We are both orphans of war although Lēofric has some distant connection to my Lord, bishop Stigand.'

She knew already, of course. The smallest lie or exaggeration would be instantly damaging.

'Stigand has been a great help to me and my husband, the king, but he continues to swim in dangerous waters. No matter. Skill and loyalty are the requirements for young men in these difficult times.

'Will you take a small refreshment?'

Goblets of wine appeared and a platter of expertly coloured delicacies shaped as nuns praying among trees in a wood. Everything was edible. I picked up a nun without sufficient thought. It was the the sweetest thing I had ever tasted. Lēofric and I were immediately hand and tongue tied as I resisted a totally inappropriate joke. This encirclement had been planned.

'Is this *marcepain*?' I asked. 'I have never tasted it before.'

She ignored my question.

'I hear from my Lord Odo that you are here to aid me in any way I wish and that you will be on hand to carry notes to him should I have need of his counsel. Do you agree?'

I nodded and she held up a hand before I could answer, my reply anticipated.

'Good, then nothing more need be said today. Your service is acceptable. If one of you is called away, for instance to Winchester, the other must remain unless I agree. A messenger who is not available is of no use to us.' She paused. The audience was at an end, but she was not quite finished.

'Is there anything that you would ask of me, cousin Gilbert?'

Was this the time for a gamble? I felt Lēofric tense beside me. Edith was surprised when I answered, her attention already moving elsewhere.

'My Lady, I have heard of your skill at embroidery. I would be grateful to see some examples of your work.'

There was a small background catching of breath.

'My beloved sister Beornthryth will show you.'

We bowed again and retreated awkwardly, hands full of wine and unfinished sweets. As the door closed, we heard a gentle ripple of laughter.

'Sometime,' said Lēofric, 'you will go too far.'

4 LOVE AND PROPAGANDA, 1069

It was a week after my visit to Edith. Ailgifu kept reining in her horse and letting out small gasps as she appreciated each new view of Winchester. As if a young child, she looked in detail at the ancient walled city for the first time. I caught her enthusiasm. At the foot of the hill, she marvelled at the twin rivers after her streamless Medstead and insisted on washing her feet, something I advised her against knowing only too well what was poured into the water. The tanners and clothmakers lived in this north east corner of the city. Gutters ran down the middle of every lane to carry away their household and industrial waste. We rode to the stone bridge built, I told her, by St Swithun when he was bishop so that the poor could cross to sell their wares in the city. I repeated the story of the crone carrying eggs to market whose goods were broken by taunting workmen. When Swithun heard, he made the sign of the cross and the eggs were made whole.

'He did many good things for poor people,' she offered.

I chose to enter by the powerful east gate where the whole glory of the straight, cobbled main thoroughfare stretched into the heart of the town. The rectangular arrangement allowed troops rapid access to any part of the walls. We dismounted and, leading the horses, slowly inspected each stretch between the six north-south streets. The walk to my house took us through a clamour from wooden houses and craft shopfronts. The noise after the quiet of the downs was shocking: the mongers' cries, the incessant chatter of small groups of soldiers and shoppers, the banging and clatter from the manufactories and the warnings from men with mules or large backpacks going about their deliveries. We bought some round flat bread and cold chicken. Above the stone wall to the left rose the Nunnaminster, the bishop's palace and the old and new minsters. We would still have been crabbing along into the night had I not promised her a tour of the minsters and the palace grounds on the next day.

Lēofric was on duty in Wilton waiting on any call from the queen. We stabled our horses, arranged for their keep, and moved straight to my upstairs lodgings. Ailgifu was the first person apart from Lēofric to be invited inside in almost two years. This seemed to please her. She took six small pots of honey from her bag.

'There you are,' she said. 'A present for your home. Three of each: clover and borage.'

She made for my chair with a cushion, that greatest of luxuries after an afternoon in the saddle. I contented myself with Lēofric's stool.

'Tell me again about Edith,' she demanded. I had met her legendary queen which was beyond her wildest imaginings. It gave me a spurious and undeserved authority especially as I had been well bested in the conversation at Wilton. For the third time, I told my story only to be frequently interrupted as she corrected small details in my account. I was quizzed deeply about the taste of marzipan, the impressive intricacies of the royal embroidery with its golden threads and the types of animals in the enclosures.

'What must it have been like as the old king died?' she mused.

'I can tell you what Goscelin wrote,' I replied. 'He gives an exciting account. The problem was that the king and queen were childless and everyone worried about what would happen when he did die. There was no mention of William. Men looked for signs and expected miracles. The king doted on Tostig, but his brother Harold was the effective power. Behind them both, the queen schemed and counselled. Stigand was seen as a devious, but powerful influence. Goscelin said the courtiers felt "the chill wind of political insecurity". The king went out of his mind with age and the queen abandoned herself to despair.'

After another burst of questions, she quietened and began to look around my rooms. She spent several minutes assessing Lēofric's small closet with its truckle bed and no window.

'All he has is a few clothes and a pile of parchment,' she said. 'Your room and bed is much better for sleeping. My brothers think I have disgraced myself by coming here. They think there can be no honour in sleeping freely with a Norman.'

I managed only a helpful gulp.

'There are rules,' she said. 'I wish to be a virgin when I marry – always if the Norman army permits. I would then be able to look at almighty God, and the faces of my dead parents, in peace. My mother always wanted me to have grandchildren. However, because of what I feel for you, pig, everything else is possible … even now if you like.'

The dam broke in a torrent. I was clumsy. I smothered her in kisses, earnestly returned, picked her up and carried her to my carefully made bed.

'I am not experienced,' I admitted.

'I think it is best to start this new relationship without an apology,' she said. 'We will have to learn together.'

It was late the next morning before she reminded me of the promised visit to the minsters and palace.

'It feels odd to be a Norman showing you around your Saxon city,' I said. I had asked many questions in the previous weeks in anticipation of her visit.

'The two main minsters are so close to each other that a man can scarcely pass between the two buildings,' I explained. 'The singers and bells of the one minster confuse and rival the singers and ringers of the other. The New Minster has this great central tower. It was dedicated over two days in the presence of king Æthelred. Wulfstan was the cantor who chanted specially prepared Latin verses.[1] I have read about this in his biography of bishop Æthelwold.'

This information got me a glance of admiration which made my heart sing and me more precocious.

'There is one thing about the two minsters that everyone knows, but apparently is never discussed,' I continued confidently. 'Lēofric explained it to me. At the conquest, the minsters took up opposite sides. The Old Minster kept close relations with the French and Norman interest, things un-English. It was the church of new ideas. The New Minister was built and established by two of the greatest English kings, Alfred and Edward, whose bones rest within its walls. It was entirely English in origin and sympathies.

'When Harold summoned an army to Hastings, the monks of the Old Minster sat on their hands. In contrast, Ælfwig, the abbot of the New Minster, led twelve monks across Swithun's bridge to the Roman road and on to the battlefield. When the fighting was over, all of them were found dead with their habits under their mail. William punished the New Minister: he took a barony for the abbot and manor for each monk, some twenty thousand acres. He refused

---

1 Cantor: a scholar monk who sings solo verses to which the choir or congregation responds.

them a new abbot for three years. He seized the upper portion of the minster's site to build his palace.'

Ailgifu was visibly shocked.

'Lēofric is from New Minster,' I added. 'And, here is your slave sanctuary. At his deathbed, Swithun ordered those standing near by to bury him outside the church where his grave would be exposed to the feet of passers-by and to the rain dripping from the eaves. Worshippers had to walk over it to get into the minster. About a hundred years ago, his stone coffin was moved and placed in a golden shrine at the high altar. Some days, it is impossible to get close, but there it is.'

All around the altar, the floor was a yellow glistening of exotic tiles reflecting the light. An early winter sun fell through densely coloured glass windows. I showed her in the walls the many courses where old Roman tiles had been reused. I explained that, when the Romans left, the town had fallen in disuse and the old streets half-disappeared beneath grass. The buildings had been robbed for material by the local people.

'Here, look, is the empty coffin, raised up and visible to all the pilgrims. If you feel inside there are hollows where the faithful are able to touch where the saint once lay.' Ailgifu stood for a long moment, sufficient for a verger to move forward to chastise her. He then saw me in my bishop's finery, and stood back. Ailgifu placed her hands in the worn groove and tears ran slowly down her cheeks.

'There have been so many miracles here,' she said.

Highly decorated biblical scenes and depictions of the lives of the saints emblazoned the walls of the Old Minster. Ailgifu was transfixed and stopped to stroke the many large stone crosses and to gaze into the secondary altars. The old site of the tomb of king Alfred, now moved to the New Minster, almost overwhelmed her.

'I did not know these drawings existed. I did not know these things could be done. We have nothing like it in our small church in Medstead. How can man have built structures so tall and so strong and then made them so beautiful? Truly, there is a God in heaven who looks down on us.' I shifted a little uneasily and kept my thoughts to myself.

That afternoon we explored the palace gardens which were not open to ordinary people. 'For me the earth is for edible plants and for feeding hogs and chickens,' she offered. 'The idea that anyone has the time to order them into collections of beautiful things just for pleasure … well, I do not know.'

The next morning we had our first disagreement as a newly declared couple. It was about getting married. I also broke a promise. Well, we both did. Our bout of lovemaking had been so ardent that the commitment to virginity at our wedding was forgotten in the passion.

As we lay back, exhausted, the realisation as to what had just happened hit us both.

'You said you wouldn't. We agreed.'

'It was your rule. You must have known what was going on.'

'You got me so excited.'

'Perhaps, we both should take some responsibility.'

'We'll have to get married very soon.'

'I would like that.'

That was the best part of the row. Later, as we walked by the river, hand in hand when no one else was close, I thought I should explain some of the new Norman law. I should have planned much better what I was going to say and, in truth, chosen another time.

I started with the easiest part. William quickly introduced to England a legal wall around the concept of dynasty. Its aim was to stop estates from being divided into equal holdings among all the children. Using the Bible as a precedent, the king introduced the primacy of the first-born male.

Ailgifu's face darkened as tight lines worked across her forehead.

'I'm not having that,' she said. 'Our women are individuals who owe nothing to any man. We can own land, run businesses, like my bees and my mead shop, and sign legal contracts. What's more, the husband must pay a morning gift after the first night, a *morgengifu*, directly to his new wife which is hers for ever. As a couple, both man and wife handle the finances of an estate and, if they divorce, they halve the holdings between them. Our custom, put into law by Cnut, specifies that on death of the husband, all his property,' and she slammed the next words into my face, 'be very justly divided among the wife and children.'

There was a brief pause as she tried to control her anger.

'So everything is taken away from me by your William,' she snorted, 'my independence, my little businesses, my land, my *morgengifu*, and my death rights.'

'It gets worse. You are going to hate this.'

I hesitated, then plunged on with the awful truth. 'Wives became property, too. Under Norman law, a married woman becomes a *feme couvert*, a covered woman, and her land, her rights, her very being, are entirely subsumed under the protective wing of her husband.'

There was an even longer pause.

'You Normans are a very backward people. So, here I am, possibly with your bastard child, and about to lose all I possess forever, to become your property if I marry you, or lose my status among my people if I do not. Well you can forget all about marriage. Is there anything else that you haven't told me?'

'Well, yes, there is. I can not get married until my Lord Odo, the bishop, consents.'

I tried my hardest to persuade her that we would work things out between us. That I loved her. That I still wanted to marry her more than anything. That we must be able to talk things through.

'Take me back to your rooms so I can get my things. Lend me a horse. I want to go home and I do not want you to come with me. You can keep the honey.'

When we arrived at the house, Lēofric was waiting, pacing up and down outside.

'Where have you been,' he almost shouted. 'I have been waiting for over an hour. Edith wants to see you immediately at Wilton.'

After protests, Ailgifu allowed Lēofric to escort her back to Medstead. She left without a word, no kiss, no glance, no future.

I was announced as soon as I arrived at the abbey.

'You are tardy, Gilbert of Bayeux.' Edith was dressed as before but seated with her surrounding nuns in more comfortable chairs. The walls were hung with tapestries that told the lives of the saints, especially Swithun. There was more evident luxury. I thought it must be her personal day room and, therefore, hinted at my gradual inclusion.

'I have ridden hard from Winchester on receiving your urgent call, my Lady.'

My answer seemed to placate her. She moved quickly to her business. She asked, not if I had read *Vita Ædwardi Regis* by the monk Goscelin, but what I thought of it.

'It is well written, my Lady. Informed and carefully drawn. It should do much to improve the reputation of your husband and his illustrious family.'

I waited to see whether I had gone too far with my flattery. I had long realised that those in power were so used to being applauded that they seldom recognised irony.

'It is a difficult journey for me, Gilbert. I am pleased with what the *Vita* seems to have achieved, but I want to go further with something more daring, something that will be a wonder of the age. I want my Lord Odo to join me in the venture and I want you to persuade him to do so. It will be greatly to his advantage. If you are successful, you will have my eternal gratitude. Everything must be in secret at the beginning.'

Edith asked whether there was anything in my life that would stop me giving my full attention to the task. I looked up at the ceiling.

'I do not mean your Saxon lover from the village past Alresford,' she said. Was there nothing this woman did not know?

'No, my Lady, you will have my full attention.'

And so, queen Edith, widow of the great Saxon king Edward, told me of her remarkable plan: to make an embroidery so long that it would stretch around a church nave. She thought Odo would delight in having such a thing for his new cathedral at Bayeux. It would tell the story, depiction by continuous depiction, of the invasion of England by William. It would be a tribute to him and his army. Everyone of importance would play their part in the history. If told correctly, Normans and Saxons could come closer together. The record would be established for ever and put in its proper place.

'Your task, Gilbert, is to make this happen. I have here a message for you to take to Odo. There will be no restriction on the money at your disposal.'

I wondered what was driving Edith to such a gesture. I assumed, as always, that she wished, foremost, to protect her fortune. Perhaps, also, she wished to rehabilitate further the name of her family, even to the extent of reinstating king Harold's sons currently in rebellion in Ireland.

It was a long cold ride to Canterbury. I found Lēofric in Winchester ready to travel. He had increased our escort to four men-at-arms because of the growing unrest across the country. During the first hour or so, I explained Edith's plan. Lēofric was impressed, excited even. We began a long discussion on how the project might be directed.

'I wonder if we will be able to influence the content,' he mused. 'The people think that the man who calls himself king is unworthy since he is a foreign bastard. Heaven has made it plain that it is not God's pleasure that such a leader should govern the kingdom. He is attacked by his own kin as much as strangers. The embroidery's job is to convince all sides.'

As we passed close to Medstead, I decided to call in to let Ailgifu know that I was away for some time in Canterbury. Then I decided against.

'I can only tell you,' shared Lēofric, 'that in my opinion the door is not completely closed, but for the moment it might as well be. She is very unhappy with Normans in general and you, being a Norman, are tainted. Generally, while I rode home with her, I kept my own counsel.'

My dilemma was solved when we met William at the Ropley crossroads, one of the small local tenants who I knew briefly from the mead shop. He agreed to pass on the message that I was in Canterbury. He gave me a queer and not very friendly look.

I thought we might have had a wasted journey for Odo was not at his lodge. The surrounding chase already looked improved and was well stocked with deer. We were directed, however, to Odo's town residence close by St Augustine's Abbey. Considerable rebuilding work was underway as the old Anglo-Saxon structure received a complete Norman restoration. The abbey, Lēofric assured me, was at the pinnacle of Anglo-Saxon worship because it contained the body of Saint Mildred, the daughter of an early Mercian king, which had been sent there by Cnut. Belief in Mildred's miraculous powers brought many pilgrims whose gifts enriched the abbey.

Odo was visible through a partly open hanging in a spartan workroom. A queue of messengers and supplicants hung around for his summons. An acolyte took in my name and Edith's letter. After a while, we moved to find some refreshment while we waited our turn. We had scarcely gone five paces when there was an urgent shout and we were called. Odo was almost dancing, clutching the letter in one hand.

'Brilliant,' he shouted. 'Brilliant. That mad woman is a genius.'

He turned to me.

'You know what this is about?' he asked and, without waiting for my reply, called for an attendant and sent him off to find Scolland, the abbot.

'Well?' he demanded.

'Yes, Lord, I had a long talk with the queen. We discussed her wishes. She has offered to provide the money. She asked me to gain your support. Then, on the road here, Lēofric and I talked through many of the practical implications. We believe that there are many benefits to everyone for such a scheme.'

'It will be the great glory of my cathedral. William will be enraptured, especially if it captures his arguments. My position will be secured against all mishaps.'

Odo grasped me by the shoulders and even spared a glance for Lēofric.

'You have done excellently, my boy. I will show my gratitude, worry not.'

Abbot Scolland bustled in, a slim, short man with skin burned brown by a distant sun. He had a freshly trimmed tonsure. His energy was arresting.

'What excitement, Lord?' he said. 'What is the urgency?'

Odo pushed Edith's letter into his hands.

'Read this, abbot, read this. Brilliant. Genius.'

After a few minutes of reading and perusal, Scolland gave his verdict.

'I agree,' he decided as he walked up and down. 'I can begin work immediately. We will recall the cause and course of the invasion at a time when it is needed. We will reinforce William's legitimate hold of the English throne. We will record the events that led up to the victory in order to provide all doubters with a vivid recreation of the victorious campaigns. It will be a careful explanation of recent history.'

Scolland turned to stand in front of Odo. 'As earl of Kent, Lord, you have access to the rich artistic heritage of Canterbury where the embroidery can be made. There is a distinguished school of needlework which can be used without delay. It can be designed here and, in part at least, in Normandy, and then taken for display in the cathedral at Bayeux.'

Scolland enhanced his case for control of the project. He was head of the Mont-Saint-Michel scriptorium which oversaw the creation and illumination of manuscripts. Both Scolland and his monks had the leading experience of the day in this kind of work. They also had first hand knowledge of William and Harold's Breton campaign which preceded the conquest.

'I would remind you, my Lord, that I have just returned from the Lateran Palace in Rome,' continued Scolland. 'It will be important that the approval given by His Highness the pope is fully recognised in order to maintain his support for our venture. In Rome, I was inspired by the triumphal monument, Trajan's Column, which commemorates the emperor's victory in the Dacian Wars.[2] The

---

2   Dacian Wars: Two military campaigns fought between the Roman Empire and Dacia during Emperor Trajan's rule in the first century. Dacia was an area north of Greece and east of the Danube.

column has a frieze which winds unbroken upward like a piece of cloth. It is a method of narration which will suit our purpose admirably.'

Scolland reached for a scrap of parchment and drew a line of five rectangles with unbroken strips top and bottom.

'You see,' he explained. 'These will portray the embroidered story in pictures. Each is joined to the next by gestures from one to another with sub-narratives above and below, the friezes, which will name the participants and add exciting detail and important background. There will be no break in the telling of the story. This *Broderie de Bayeux* should not be tall, but long enough to encircle the whole nave of the cathedral.'

Odo clapped in delight. For my part, it was breathtaking to see such an important idea given life in minutes with resources identified and brought into play.

'Gilbert, how will this sit with queen Edith? Did you have other ideas while on your ride here?'

I paused to get my thoughts into order.

'The queen will be anxious to stay involved and to know that her requirements for content will be included. She will worry when she hears that at least part of the design is to be led from Mont-Saint-Michel and that the main embroidery is to undertaken here in Canterbury rather than Wilton or Winchester. I would respectfully remind you that she sees this as her project, indeed it is her initial idea, and that she expects to pay for it.

'May I suggest, Lord, that, unless you wish the queen to arrive in Canterbury to provide a stream of advice, we devise a method to keep her involved, but separate from day-to-day work. For your consideration, I suggest that I remain closely involved, perhaps travelling back and forth each month with copies drawn on parchment or linen for her review. I also know that she has some clear requirements. For instance, she wishes the story to start when king Edward sends his brother-in-law, Harold, on a mission to France. She wants to be shown tending to king Edward on his death bed. She also wishes to appear on her throne in tears following the royal demise. She does not wish Harold to be shown other than dying an heroic death.'

Odo looked at me deeply and said, 'Well advised, my faithful Gilbert. You will liaise with queen Edith. We need her compliance and her enthusiastic agreement to keep the Saxons happy.'

'That also means, Lord, that she will wish to see the completed piece. There would be an advantage, showing deference to her perceived position, to carry it to her in Wilton or Winchester before it is taken onward to Bayeux. There may be other opportunities for display because of this transfer, for your consideration, of course.'

'Your advice is invaluable, Gilbert.' He stopped and gazed at Lēofric. 'Your man, here, Lēofric isn't it? He is a Saxon, well spoken for, but a Saxon all the same and a relative of bishop Stigand who has long experience, but who has played a scheming role in the succession. Stigand's time for reckoning is coming. We have spoken very openly here. There will be choices to make with the history. How does your man stand? Can you continue to trust him?'

'Speak, Lēofric,' I commanded.

'My Lord,' he said, 'I am bound to Gilbert as his servant and adviser, a role given to me by Hugh de Port and gladly accepted over the past two years. Both Gilbert and Hugh de Port are your men, therefore I am also. I would also remind your Lordship of the silent role I played in the disposition of the estates of the thegns fallen at Hastings.'

'That is also well said,' replied Odo. 'Your obedience is as welcome as your skills. You must keep it that way for the alternative would be unpleasant.'

Lēofric bowed gracefully, just the right touch of obsequiousness I thought, and then continued. For a moment he had me worried.

'Initially, my Lord, and even later, the hanging may not be limited to one location. Court life is mobile. The work may need to be transported to be admired by more viewers. Textiles can travel safely, wrapped in waxed linen covers. I suggest that when all the measuring is done and the number of drawings that are needed to fit Bayeux cathedral exactly is known, a further estimate is made to have it housed snugly in a purpose-built and elegant chest. This can also be used for storage when necessary. Weight will also be important.

'If you will excuse me further, Lord, there is an associated matter which may seem trivial currently, but which I believe will later carry great importance. The size of a chest to be moved by men and on a wagon and placed on a boat will determine not so much the length of the embroidery, but its height. It will need to be manageable, perhaps slightly less than an outstretched arm. This will affect all our early planning.'

Lēofric bowed gracefully again.

'You pair continue to delight me,' concluded Odo. 'Let us eat on it and discuss some more.'

The meal was a surprise for Adam was visiting from Dover to report on progress at the castle. Vital and Wadard were with him and the three had formed a close relationship. They were part of the inner circle and the plan for a masterpiece of embroidery was shared. The excitement among these warriors over a piece of textile was palpable. The targets were agreed: beauty, vigour of design, skill of execution and a wealth of historical detail. All of us would appear, drawn by needle and thread, and this would be for our private amusement.

Towards the end of the meal, abbot Scolland took me to one side. He told me Odo had asked that I be given some extra information in private about church matters.

'These thoughts are so that you are not surprised by what happens and are ready for any reaction from queen Edith. We do not want our newly-born project upset at its very beginning.'

I nodded in gratitude and bided my time.

'William came to England as a self-avowed reformer with a record of modernisation in the Norman church and the approval of the pope behind him. His succession was agreed by Edward and by Harold until he broke his word. This is the truth that will be expressed in Odo's ornament for the walls of his new cathedral.'

I nodded, this time in agreement.

'Even now at William's request, the pope has sent his three legates, Ermenfrid, Peter and John Minutus, to England with the task of reforming the English clergy. Their first task will be to assist in William's recrowning which will confirm direct papal authority.

'Next, the legates will declare the sins of the English church at a special Council. They will uphold the accusations of plurality, the holding of the sees of both Canterbury and Winchester against bishop Stigand. Stigand will be imprisoned in Winchester and two other English bishops dismissed for simony, the buying or selling of ecclesiastical privileges, for example pardons or benefices. Finally, all the clergy across the land will be accused of laziness and avarice, prolonged vacancies in monasteries, open receipt of payments for church appointments, accumulated church leases and the collection of treasure.

'Note these offences are not political misconduct or sedition, all of which could be proved if we chose, but ecclesiastical crimes condemned by the pope. We will seek suitable penances by way of expiation, gifts to churches and the founding of new religious houses as part recompense from the clergy at large.

'Stigand's replacements are already agreed: the saintly Lanfranc of Bec will take Canterbury and the primacy of the church in England; Walkelin who is of noble birth and is related to William will hold Winchester. You should know that Walkelin is a canon at Rouen, where he is called *Vauquelin*, and where sits the head of the Norman church. He is a tough and unforgiving man. If you are called upon to make choices, step very carefully and keep your man Lēofric under tight control when in his presence.'

I nodded acceptance.

'You should now understand that this is the next stage in the subjugation of the English. The new Norman bishops will align the church with the conquest. There will be no more appointments of local men to English bishoprics. Every priest in England will be directed to invite the people to hear three masses for the king's health and to shorten his time in purgatory. Anyone who speaks treason against William will be excommunicated.'

Scolland weighed up whether to continue and decided I could be trusted.

'There is a danger,' he said. 'The appointment of these and later bishops will stretch our resources in Normandy, especially with the threats there to the dukedom. Some of these new men will not be chaste, nor religious, nor even educated.'

'That is a lot to assimilate, abbot,' I replied, thinking of my earlier self-pledge not to become dangerously involved in the politics and greed of great men.

'You are clutching at the tail of a headstrong beast,' said Scolland. 'Do not be fooled into believing you can in any way control it. Salvation lies in doing your duty.'

He then paused and told me that I had one additional task. When Stigand was imprisoned, I was to visit him with Lēofric in the hope that his tongue might be loosened. Any disconcerting news I gathered on the changes to the church, or on insurrection, either from Stigand or from Edith, should be reported during my regular visits to Canterbury to allow countermeasures and to guard the production of the Bayeux embroidery.

Scolland blessed me and left me to my thoughts which were many and mostly frightening. I collected Lēofric who grinned at me.

'It seems we have a job for the next few years, my Lord Gilbert. And, importantly, as we act as intermediaries between two confident men, we will have plenty of opportunity to influence the content of this masterpiece. Our names may yet go down in legend.'

'Your enthusiasm may be premature, my friend,' I replied. 'We are about to walk on a tightrope and there will be no safety net if we slip.'

5 CAREFUL WHAT YOU ASK FOR, 1070

Lēofric and I rode back to Winchester somewhat slower than usual. We needed to travel side by side to be able to talk. There were two topics.

First, we wanted to examine the implications of the various plots and sub-plots in which Odo and his men had involved us. We were increasingly mired in the bishop's world although not as innocents for I, certainly, owed my increasing wealth to his avarice. At one level, everything seemed simple enough, but at another we recognised that we were the expendable links in the middle of the chain, capable of being blamed from any direction. We had begun to think of our world almost entirely in terms of 'them' and 'us'.

Second, evidence was all around on the road from Canterbury through lonely villages in Surrey and into Hampshire that we were part of an army of occupation. Most of the lands off the main roads had still never seen a full Norman patrol. William and his followers were a tiny minority of the total population, 25,000 in two million was the guess. Three years after Hastings, few people, certainly not the everyday soldiery, knew how vulnerable we were to a determined uprising and being thrown back whence we came. William knew and sent his wife Matilda, now crowned queen of England, and their first son, Robert, to safety in Normandy. Security was the continuing concern and repression the only response.

The disconnect began with the devastation of land along the coast to Canterbury immediately after the conquest. Then came the mutilation of a hostage at Exeter. In Hampshire and Kent we were only dimly aware of what was going on in the far north where much of the countryside and most of the towns and villages were subject to ruthless suppression.

Our party had just reached the ridge above the beech trees of Chawton when we were met by a small group of curiously armed men from Medstead. They were led by one of Ailgifu's brothers, Isen, whom I recognised from the mead shop. He carried a longbow while others clutched pitchforks and cudgels. We drew swords and readied to fight or flee, but as Isen stepped forward with his hands outstretched in peace, I realised they were waiting for us, or to be precise, for me.

Ailgifu would like to meet with me urgently. Would I come to the mead shop, the place of most comfort in the hamlet? Our safety was guaranteed. My men-at-arms weighed the odds and disappeared into the dusk.

'There was no chance that you were going to turn down that invitation,' said Lēofric as we followed our escort. One of the men raced ahead so that Ailgifu was waiting at the door to her shop. I do not know what I expected: invective, embarrassment, but it was certainly not a wild rush into my arms. She was crying. We walked to the side of the building to the rubble of a Roman villa and stood on the remains of a large mosaic, a regular pattern of crosses which held intricate depictions of fabulous beasts. We were alone, but closely watched.

'You must help me. My younger brother, Kent, the wild one, has been taken by the soldiers at our fort to Winchester. He is accused of murder of a Norman. I know he is innocent. You must save him. I fear they may hang him tonight.'

After a few minutes of convoluted question and answer, I got close to what had happened. The soldiers heard cries from the woods and sent a small patrol which found a king's messenger, a crossbow arrow protruding from his back. He died as they reached him. Hearing a crashing in the undergrowth, they gave chase, startling a small deer, and then, hiding under a bush, found Kent holding a crossbow. He was arrested, accused, protested his innocence, but was taken off to the capital.

'How do you know he didn't do it?' I asked.

'Because here is the arrow from the body,' she said. 'It is not his. He was out after deer. We are hungry for meat in Medstead as we also have the soldiers to feed.'

It was a bad situation all ways, I thought. It was likely the sheriff, Hugh de Port, would want to make a quick example. There were very few acts of violence in the area and he would want to stamp quickly on any contagion before it spread. There was enough good evidence, but Kent's guilt or otherwise would not be his main concern. One dead Saxon was much like another. Even if Kent was innocent, he had already admitted to trying to poach the king's deer and that was punishable by blinding. The only possible loophole I could see was that he had not killed any game.

The light had almost gone from the sky as we walked back to the shop. The group of angry and frightened men threw muddied shadows in front of the hearth while they grumbled together. Lēofric had dismounted and was holding the reins of our horses while his other hand rested on the hilt of his sword. I told him the story.

'We need to leave quickly if we are to get to Winchester before the matter is settled without us,' he suggested.

'I will do what I can,' I told Ailgifu, 'but your troubles may only just be starting. Under the law of murdrum, the responsibility for finding the murderer rests with the men of Medstead and if no one is offered up you may lose whatever money you have and your land.'

We mounted and rode away over the rough ground as quickly as was sensible. By Winchester, I had a plan which filled me with a particular horror. I found Hugh, as expected, at the castle prison. Kent was hanging by chains from an iron ring in a bloodied wall trying to balance his pain against his last shreds of dignity. A whip cracked as we entered the room and Kent screamed. Hugh saw us and waved.

'Come to see the fun?' he asked. 'This viper was caught in the act of murdering a king's messenger.' Hugh was in a good mood, evidently having just finished his meal. He held a large goblet of wine.

'A word please, sheriff?' I requested.

I led him out of earshot of the others and told him all that I knew. I then played my only card.

'I do not know this man well,' I said, 'but I am assured that he is innocent.'

Hugh shrugged. 'Does it really matter?' he asked.

'It is an affair of the heart,' I replied. 'This man is the brother of the woman I wish to marry. His death would not further my plans. I am asking you as a personal favour to hand him over to me and set him free.'

'A king's messenger is dead,' he retorted. 'We must be strong lest these reptiles overwhelm us.'

'Nevertheless, Hugh, you are a resourceful man. I believe I have been useful to you and could be more so. At least sleep on it and see if a solution comes to light in the morning.'

Much of Norman culture is clouded by the many and varied relationships which exist between men of power. The king was always the king, but it was not a rigid pyramidal structure, more a series of personal relationships with lords owing and receiving multiple obligations. These often criss-crossed and occasionally contradicted. I could see the light change in Hugh's eyes as he saw the benefit of another favour owed.

'Blast you, Gilbert, you've ruined my evening. Come and see me tomorrow at midday and I'll see what can be done.'

'I am on a mission, Hugh, carrying a commission from my Lord Odo to queen Edith. I will be able to share in confidence information of a great move afoot.'

He looked up at me. The deal was struck.

Hugh caught sight of Lēofric talking quietly to Kent and called him over.

'Do you know the man?' he asked.

'I have seen him in the background, Lord,' he replied. 'I know his sister better because she is a fancy of my Lord Gilbert.'

'Well, I have an instruction for you, Lēofric,' he said. 'Those two pots of honey you sent to me I passed to the king. I can not stand the stuff myself, too sweet. William is enamoured with one of them; I hear the bees feast on a plant called borage to make it. He has asked for more. As you'll no doubt be going back to the source, you can fulfil the royal wishes.'

Lēofric bowed and we made our exit.

'A Saxon life for a pot of honey,' he quipped. 'Ironic. What did you offer?'

'A different sort of honey,' I replied through gritted teeth.

Next day, I saw Hugh at his luxurious palace rooms. There were as many personal servants as wall hangings and quilted high-backed chairs.

'You will be pleased, I think,' he said. 'You were right. The arrows were different, but that means, of course, that the man could be blinded for poaching from our noble king. A solution has been found at great speed by Oda, my dapifer at Chawton. He suggests that the woods were probably on the edge of his land and not at Medstead. By chance, he had a surly fellow from his manor just taken into lock up. This incident offered him the opportunity to rid himself of an irritation.'

Hugh told me that I would no doubt see this troublemaker and undoubted murderer swinging from some local tree when I next visited my Saxon sweetheart.

'All ended well, then,' he said. 'Justice done. Norman supremacy projected. Local peasants in fear of the next time. Your girl happy with you and, hopefully, very grateful. Now what is it that I need to know about my lord bishop and the queen, Edith?'

I explained the embroidery project. Hugh was delighted with the idea. He urged me to ensure that his own prominent part in the invasion was properly recorded. He wanted everyone to know that he was a hero.

'Remember, Gilbert, I take my debts most seriously. I will be calling on you one day. I know I will be able to count on you. Get Lēofric to pick up the pile of shit from the gaoler and take him home. If I see this brother again, I will skewer him myself.'

Kent had to be washed in vinegar and water and wrapped in a winding bandage as ribs seemed broken. His nose was flattened to his face and I did not like the look of his right eye. His mouth was too damaged to eat and we forced his lips apart to give him beer. His clothes were burned and replaced. Then we tied him to a horse and Lēofric took him to Medstead at a crawl. He told me later that it took over three hours. When he arrived he found the mood mixed and worrying: surprise at the rapid release, jubilation at the homecoming, anger at the state of Kent's body, applause for Lēofric's care, hatred and fear of the Norman conquerors, gratitude for what I had managed, and utter dismay that all had been achieved at the cost of the life, callously disposed, of a probably innocent man from Chawton.

Lēofric felt there was some hidden secret, perhaps a plan of retaliation or knowledge of who the attacker had been. He was well fed and feted with mead as Kent was carried to a bed with several women in attendance. Ailgifu came to see Lēofric and thank him personally and asked him to give me the message that I would be welcome when I next passed by. She also handed over several pots of borage honey from Ropley at his request, the new favourite of the king she despised. She refused payment.

Meanwhile, I left *Thor* to rest and took a new horse from the castle stable to ride at a steady pace to Wilton. The road to Sarum was not considered dangerous and I went alone. Perhaps my great achievement to date was in just staying alive, I mused. For an orphan boy, I had risen to a useful status among powerful men. Was this the sort of life I wished to lead? It seems my Norman masters were a race that embraced war and scarcely know how to live without it. Thank God, by chance, I had not been trained for battle and slaughter. I was already sickened by what I had seen and knew. I had increasing sympathy with the English and, if discovered, that consideration would see me cast out. Did I want to change my work and settle with Ailgifu if she would ever have me? To do what? To bring children into this unstable existence? And where: Medstead, Winchester or near Bayeux? There was no safe place in my world.

I realised that I stood on the edge of great events. I was within the circle of people who knew much of what was in the minds of the few who ruled the country. I now knew without doubt that the continuing rebellions had persuaded William to dispossess English landowners on a massive scale. What was more, he had decided that he was entitled to do this and he welcomed support from any quarter for his claim of a legitimate succession. Estates were given to new owners, often by word of mouth. It was chaotic. Nobody even knew how big England was or, in detail, who owned what.

However, Saxons like Ailgifu knew the recent history of the land and its previously shared ownership. She was no lover of the Normans.

I took the old Roman Road from Winchester to Sarum because I wanted to visit the stone castle that was growing there. The motte and bailey with its strong curtain wall was thrown up a few years ago on top of an old hillfort. The new castle was held directly by William because it controlled the intersection of three trade routes and the River Avon. There were plans for a cathedral. It was an impressive place rising in the morning sun from the flat plains. No one could approach without notice. It looked impregnable. Workmen swarmed over its sides. On both sides of the wall, a small town bustled with endeavour. A market meant the roads were clogged with cattle and carts carrying vegetables, chickens, crafts and weapons, all vying for right of passage with trains of building material.

Castles were scarcely known in the provinces, but it was the Norman way: extensive castle building and permanent garrisons. After riding to all parts of his new kingdom, William put up a trail of newly-proven fortresses along his route. He appointed strong men as their guardians and introduced rich fiefs that induced them to endure toil and danger to defend them. The English, despite their love of fighting, never tried to take them.

The knight was the essential element of William's military power: crop headed, mounted on well-trained and specially-bred horses, heavily equipped, clad in chain mail, used to fighting on horseback with throwing and jabbing lances and cutting swords, accustomed to operating in squadrons, to act in concert, to respond to the movement of flags, to use archer cover, expert and ruthless in breaking up and routing a defeated host, accustomed to devastation as one of the inevitable results of war. The Saxons' old tactics failed as at Hastings. Although their densely packed, heavily armed infantry resisted behind their efficient shield walls they were eventually broken through ill-discipline or the sheer weight of cavalry and were slaughtered by the knights. Until a prayed-for army of invasion appeared in the north, resistance fighters were driven to the woods and marshes to ambush and run, always on the move.

After a day's wait and rest for which I was grateful, my meeting with Edith was prompt and short. She was delighted with the progress I had made and reluctantly accepted that responsibility for the production of the embroidery would lie with people she did not know in Canterbury and Mont-Saint-Michel. However, I stressed the importance that everyone placed on her playing a pivotal role in the development of the story. With her sisters and ladies, she had already developed a vivid style of presentation which she showed to me in three examples. She stressed the use of embroidery on linen rather than tapestry work to bring a bold and lively sense of movement. I congratulated her and promised to take her suggestions the next week to Canterbury. As I left with my marzipan, she told me that the papal legates had arrived at Winchester. They were beginning the sham of hearing evidence at a Great Council. She feared for bishop Stigand.

'Also, Gilbert, I do insist that I see the fruit of all our ideas before it leaves for Bayeux. I charge you to bring it to me for my approval before the king sees it or it leaves the country.'

'Of course, my Lady,' I replied, 'although it will be too late to make any changes.'

She looked up at me and waved her silk embroidery bag which contained all the sharp tools of her skill.

'Your discretion and loyalty as always, Gilbert.' I was dismissed.

Lēofric greeted me, agitated, with a ragbag of important news. I felt he would be a long time getting to the point. Kent had been safely delivered and all was quiet. Some pots of honey had been delivered to William's chamberlain and had been acknowledged. The old priest who lived below had died and his wife departed so Lēofric had, on his own initiative, taken the whole house as I 'would soon be getting married' and he could take a larger room downstairs looking out over the small garden. This would make a pleasant place for a newly-wed couple to sit out on warm evenings to which end he had employed a gnarled old farm hand to do some gentle planting and trimming.

'Do you know that bishop Stigand has been arrested?' he asked. 'According to the royal plan, of course. He has been found guilty of plurality. I hear his cell at the castle is comfortable enough. He has books, but few visitors apart from monks from his order. People are wary of being tainted by association.'

'Too fast,' I interjected. 'What do you mean about me getting married? My prospects there are dismal.'

'Well, I think the affair with young Kent will no doubt have helped your cause. But the message I have been asked to carry is that all the fault lies with the king and his invading pigs. Underneath your great misfortune of being a Norman, you have a pleasant side to your nature. It is not my place, you know, Lord, but I should not delay in pressing your suit next time you pass by Medstead. If I may, just let Ailgifu know that you are on your way to Canterbury to ask for my Lord Odo's permission, so that you are ready if she changes her mind about your offer.

'When we get back, we can make an arrangement to visit Stigand for Odo and see what he is plotting.'

I sat back and had a long drink. That was a lot of change to cram into one half hour, but, as I suspected, Lēofric had not yet finished.

'I have heard more about the horrors of the North where William has been campaigning,' he said. 'Information has been coming to Winchester slowly, but faster through English connections who can scarce believe what has been done in the name of God and king. It is being called the "harrowing".'

Lēofric roughed out the story for me. Local resistance had grown in the north and their leaders were in constant negotiation to secure help from Denmark and Scotland. Rebels in Yorkshire joined with Danish invaders. The Normans lost control of York and there were uprisings in the Midlands and the West Country. There were regular raids by the Irish Vikings into the deep inlets of Devon and Cornwall.

Edgar, a kinsman of king Edward, challenged William's claim to the throne with the backing of the Scottish king, Malcolm. In a brutal campaign, fire, rape, and daily slaughter brought destruction, starvation and disaster on all the wretched people. William turned a vast tract into a wilderness with no inhabited place left between York and Durham. Refugees streamed north into Scotland leading to the Englishing of the Lowlands. Exiles and misfits washed up on the shores of Ireland, Flanders and Denmark.

William then threatened to invade Scotland. Malcolm withdrew and Edgar fled.

'Everywhere the law of God was broken,' said Lēofric as he began to cry in a mixture of impotence and hate. He began to babble. 'The king cut down many people and destroyed homes and land. Crops, herds, tools and food were burned to ashes. Nowhere else had he shown such cruelty. William made no effort to control his fury, punishing the innocent with the guilty. Souls were imperilled by the sins of envy and anger and in their thousands swept away to Hell. And, do you know, he took his wife with him and in the middle of all this she gave him a fourth son, Henry. God will punish him.' [*When we came to the great survey in 1086, we found over 1,300 places that were wasted of which over 1,000 came from five northern counties.*]

Lēofric arrived at his main personal worry.

'William has announced the northern rebellion as the time and reason to stop using English officials and servants,' he said, 'although we always knew that this was his plan. We are to be thrown out. My place here in Winchester with you is in great danger. Remember how Odo threatened me in Canterbury just a few days ago. I will soon be no longer needed.'

I poured him another glass and tried to reassure him although what security could I offer? I told Lēofric that Odo had every opportunity to warn me off, but he had not. I would discuss matters with Odo when we next went to Canterbury. Hugh de Port also had a chance in a time of stress, but instead gave Lēofric an errand to fetch honey for the king. I was sure that the royal circle did not mean to cast out Englishmen who were assisting messengers and clerks like me. Otherwise why would we be asked to work with Edith and to visit Stigand?

We got maudlin and drank deep into the night.

After an hour or so, I told Lēofric that I had one story to cheer him up. Edith had demanded to see the embroidery at Wilton when it was finished. She fully intended to make immediate, clandestine alterations if there was anything she did not like. Using her own undoubted skills and those of her companions, it is unlikely that any changes would ever be noticed.

Lēofric laughed at that.

'But do you see?' I said. 'This means that as we carry the demands for content from one side to the other, we will always put the responsibility for the requests on those not in the room. No one will check our motives. No one will ever know if we decide to add to the story to suit our own purposes. There will be space for Ailgifu and for you and me.

'Even if you are thrown out into the street, you will still have pride of place in the Norman's greatest work of art and will hang in Bayeux Cathedral to be marvelled at by men for all time!'

In the early morning, still giggling like children, we fell asleep.

6 STIGAND'S DEFENCE, 1071

Abbot Scolland was pleased with Edith's embroidery suggestions. The dimensions of Bayeux's cathedral nave were brought by messenger that evening. We sat down with charcoal and parchment and made the calculations. The nave circumference allowed for about sixty scenes which, if they were to present a seamless flow, needed to be planned in advance of the attentions of the seamstresses. The scenes would have to be approved by Odo and by Edith. Scolland set his clerks to work on manufacturing the linen and collecting sufficient quantities of vibrantly dyed woollen threads. To my surprise, Scolland insisted that the threads came from Winchester where the Romans had set up a large dyeing workshop over one thousand years before. Its wool was the most prized in Europe. It was here, he said, that that the best quality woad, weld, madder and greenweed could be found.

Scolland was also happy with Edith's other ideas. She thought that the English should be differentiated from the Normans and that this was best done by emphasising their moustaches and long, combed oiled hair. The tightly cropped Normans called the English 'ladyboys' so the result did not always produce the respect that Edith intended. The Normans were to be called 'Franci', that is 'Franks' or 'Frenchmen'. I am not sure now, but I think this was to disassociate them from their raiding, pagan ancestors.

Edith had her way. In fact there was no dispute. The draft story began with a bearded, enthroned king Edward commanding his brother-in-law Harold Godwinson to visit William in Normandy. There he would pledge his loyalty to the Norman duke as designated successor to the English crown.

'That's a lie in the very first scene,' claimed Lēofric, grumbling behind my back. 'Everyone knows Harold was sent to gain the release of kinsmen held by William as hostages. Why is Edith accepting a lie about what her brother was doing?'

'This is, perhaps, the trade off,' I suggested. 'We did not see what deal Edith offers Odo in the letter we carried. She does not claim in her book that Edward promised the throne to Harold. She agrees that Harold went to Normandy to accept William as his future king. All the possible gainsayers except Stigand are now dead. Reinforcing any alternative view will only bring futile strife. By doing what she has done, she confirms William and, in return, keeps her rank, her lands and her treasure.'

The Norman view was reinforced in the next scenes when Harold was shown riding with six men to his estate at Bosham on the Solent to take ship. It is an exciting tale. Their peaceful intent is reinforced by their lack of armour and the number of hounds and a hawk intended as ducal gifts. Harold's party is shown praying and feasting. A favourable wind turns bad after sailing; they wreck on the French coast where the hostile count Guy of Ponthieu captures them. They will likely be sold as slaves or killed. One man escapes, reaches William's court, and messengers are sent demanding Harold's release. Harold stays with William for some time, even participating in a military expedition against the Bretons in which he saves soldiers' lives by pulling them from quicksand. The Normans are impressed. Late in this period, a scene at Bayeux shows Harold making his famous and fateful oath. There is no suggestion of duress, indeed all is sweetness as the oath, claimed the Normans, was the purpose of the mission.

Edward died in early January in his new church at Westminster and the very next day, before the funeral meats were cold, Harold seized the throne and was crowned in the abbey. As the embroidery makes clear, at least to Norman eyes, Harold was now a perjurer. William's claim was legitimate. The scene is set for the battle at Hastings.

Scolland set me two tasks on top of my liaising with Edith. I had been in Normandy at first hand during the preparations for the invasion fleet. He asked me to draw up a series of scenes depicting this work. He also wanted a list of all those who were party to the production and to give my thoughts as to how they could be included in the narrative. This second task was meat and drink to my more frivolous plans for Ailgifu, Lēofric and myself.

I asked for an audience with Odo who Scolland told me was at Canterbury. Now Stigand was deposed, the renowned Lanfranc had arrived from Caen to take up his bishopric and was receiving visitors. In two days, there was to be a celebratory mass followed by a feast in the cathedral building which was much damaged by a recent fire. An invitation could be arranged for me, but Scolland suggested Lēofric would be out of place.

Scolland was inclined to gossip.

'Lanfranc is an old man and really an academic,' he told me. 'He is a Lombard, not even a Norman. He revitalised the abbey school at Bec and, as a result, is a close friend to pope Alexander. What will he achieve amidst the war and politics of England? He has already told me that he sees so much unrest and distress in the country that he only expects matters to get worse.

'Still he is William's man; he was his counsellor when he was head of Abbaye-aux-Hommes at Caen and also argued with the pope for William's illegal marriage. Lanfranc will concern himself more with the working of his cathedral and with the upper echelons of the clergy than with the population at large. He wants to keep the leaders pure and simple, but I suspect he will end by separating them from the sullying effects of day-to-day life.'

He paused and then shared, 'Odo is already worried for himself as he should be.'

Scolland thought Lanfranc was a great builder.

'You watch him when he sets to work on the new cathedrals like Winchester. Look at what he has achieved already after the great fire at the cathedral in Canterbury. You do not know what to admire more, the beauty or the speed. It will be interesting for you to compare him to Stigand when you visit him in prison.'

I was taken aback. Here was another Norman who knew much more about my business than I expected.

The mass at Canterbury was a dull affair and so was the meal that followed. Lanfranc's personality did not fill a space as did Stigand by reputation. The new archbishop had little to say of note. He accepted that kings and bishops shared jointly in the governance of the church, but it was the king's duty to protect the church especially when he carried a heavy burden of sin brought about by his violent lifestyle. This was not as daring as it may sound from a man who knew William well. It was actually a demand for increased funding. William could make amends by generous gifts to the church. This was followed by a sop to the barons and their followers: a good lord should be generous to them, respecting their rights and protecting their lands.

Lanfranc did announce that he would shortly leave for Rome to collect his symbolic pallium, the scarf-like woollen vestment of office. This was a pointed dig at Stigand who never received his own pallium, but was excommunicated instead for his pluralism. Of interest to me was that Lanfranc was to be accompanied by Thomas, the new archbishop of York, for the same purpose. Thomas arrived to find his cathedral church destroyed in the northern rebellion. Like Lanfranc, Thomas was a builder and educator. Rebuilding was advanced and the new school was quickly gaining a reputation as a great producer of scholars and effective clerks.

I sought out Odo and found him after the meal surrounded by a small knot of his placemen, including Thomas, and stood respectfully at a distance waiting for a summons. I could overhear Thomas arguing his belief that York was a see independent of Canterbury and, especially, Lanfranc. After an appropriate delay, Odo called me into a private huddle as he was anxious to hear first hand of developments on the embroidery. To my surprise, Thomas recognised me from when he had interviewed me a long time ago in a bare room in Bayeux. He was another of Odo's men who had been sponsored as a youth with his brother Samson to the renowned Liège School.

'Ah, the kitchen boy with the gift of tongues,' he declared. 'Have you added English to your list of achievements?'

I bowed slightly and told him that it was in daily use.

'Valuable, valuable, and what services are you now performing for my Lord Odo?'

Odo explained my work liaising with Edward's queen. It was clear Thomas was already well aware of what I was doing. My brief update obviously chimed with what they already knew from Scolland.

'And you will be seeing the religious hypocrite Stigand shortly,' added Odo. 'We will all be interested to hear what he has to say. He is ignoring all requests for information from his interrogators.'

It was time for another bow from me. 'If I could, my Lord,' I said, to Odo, 'a brief, private matter ...' I let my words trail away.

Odo looked me square in the eye. 'Do not tell me you wish to get married? Have you been making extra use of your new tongue?'

'My Lord is ahead of me as always. The lady ...'

Odo cut me off. 'The lady who has a brother who carries a crossbow which could be used to assassinate king's messengers?'

'I can assure you, my Lord, ...'

'What do you think, Thomas, would it be too dangerous to let this pup on heat have his way with a local girl, granddaughter of a notorious thegn who switched his loyalty between Saxon and Danish kings and back again?'

Thomas enjoyed my discomfiture and then gave his verdict. 'I think, my Lord Odo, that Gilbert of Bayeux has given loyal service to you on a number of important matters. He well understands, I'm sure, how unfortunate your displeasure would be for his prospects and that of a new family. Marriages between French men and English women are now quite common and have the blessing of the king, especially when they help resolve any disputes over land. I would give your useful servant your permission and your blessing.'

'There, you have it,' said Odo. I bowed and left quickly to the sound of gentle laughter.

I recounted Odo's exact words to Lēofric as we rode west the next day, well wrapped against the bitter cold.

'It's quite clear that you are not in any immediate danger,' I told him. 'What Odo and Thomas were saying is that you and I are being closely watched. So, do not think you can say or do something that could be taken as disloyal and expect Odo not to hear of it. He is on the edge of major disagreement with Lanfranc and is worried about the security of all his property acquisitions and his projects. He is more the earl of Kent than he ever is a bishop.'

'Projects like his damned embroidery,' spat Lēofric. 'It's all a pack of lies and what's more it will probably work. If the story is in pictures hanging from a church wall, people will believe it. He will be forever in the king's favour. I am not sure at all I still want my name on the thing.'

'Now, there I had an idea,' I replied. 'I think it's something that will appeal to you.'

I leaned over and whispered in his ear. After a few minutes, he broke into a great grin.

'Perfect,' he said. 'Absolutely perfect.'

'Good. That's agreed. However, it is also clear that Odo now sees me as useful because you and I act as a pair. An Englishman and a Norman working closely together have some distinct advantages. I do not think we were brought together by Hugh by accident. On the one hand, our national tensions may be supposed to keep us in check. On the other, we provide more acceptable and useful access to, say, the land records, queen Edith, and to Stigand.'

I reflected a while longer in silence and then shared my thoughts.

'However, it is obvious that I am still not completely trusted. I have an English servant who lives with me independently in the town. We both speak each other's languages and can switch easily between them. Hopefully, I am to take an English wife but her family are suspected assassins. We need to watch each other's back.'

My four men-at-arms had been replaced by soldiers made of sterner stuff. These young men took the risks and their responsibilities much more seriously, riding at all times with a pair well in front to guard against ambush and two behind. I took the change from casual social outings as evidence that someone, I suspected Hugh, had taken disciplinary measures. It was noticeable how alert the men became as we entered Chawton woods. And yet, for all our unplanned schedule, Ailgifu was at the door with a broad smile as we approached the comfort of her shop. We both received embraces and her extended family came outside to slap our shoulders.

'How is Kent?' I asked.

'He is much subdued and still resting in his cot. I believe that he was very frightened and he has not yet recovered a manly gait. His ribs are mending, but he does not have full sight in one eye. We are hopeful. He sends his thanks as do we all.'

Lēofric went inside into the warmth while Ailgifu and I walked slowly around the pond. Some ice had formed, broken where cattle had been to drink. A few ducks were confined to a patch of free water in the middle. The bare rush stalks overhanging one bank were rimed with a day-long frost. On one, a robin sat and waited.

We broke the silence at the same time. 'I wanted to …; I thought that …'

In the end, I just asked her to marry me and she said, 'Of course.' A pause. 'I would like it to be soon although there is no rush. There is no baby. I am disappointed. What about Odo?'

'He has given his permission as also has the new bishop of York who was with him. You could say that we are twice blessed. He knows of you and your grandfather.'

After a pause, I asked, 'Have you talked with your family? Are they opposed?'

'There is nothing to worry about there. They accept I will move to Winchester. They are keen to visit. The shop and the bees will be in good hands and I thought that, sometimes, when you pass by here, I could come with you and stay till you return. Hopefully, it will all mean better days for everyone.'

We embraced and there were muted cheers in the background.

She asked what Odo had said about her grandfather and I told her of his sour reputation. She became reflective and quiet.

'It is mostly true,' she said, 'but I can explain more at another time.'

We discussed arrangements briefly. I offered her a marriage contract outside the Old Minster near to St Swithun's grave site. She found the idea exciting, but declined, deciding to use the porch of her small parish church where her parents had wed and where the people she grew up with could easily attend. We agreed the first Saturday in February, two weeks away, and I would bring only Lēofric who would arrange and send sufficient food and drink.

'No Normans, then?'

'No, no Normans.'

I said I would like one piece of information. It was not to cause dissension, but only so that I would be better able to protect her. I needed to know what land she held and who was her lord.

'Of course, husband,' she said. She held my hand and with me in tow paced out a plot around the shop. She took me towards a slight hill and showed me a stretch of land fenced with wattle containing two pigs and three cows. She pointed to the other side and said she held six strips on the common land where the villagers grew barley and root vegetables. She also held two acres for clover bees in Medstead which I had seen and another two acres in Ropley for her borage bees and which had belonged to her mother. She told me how I could find the hives. All the land had been hers by right, given by her father, but it now belonged to the king. All her property was leased from the church at Winchester and the bishop was Walkelin now Stigand was in gaol. The church's steward did not bother her much as long as she paid her fees on time and gave him free mead for the favour.

'Will you stay the night?'

'You know I would love to, but I can not. I have an important meeting tomorrow with the old bishop, Stigand. Lēofric and I have been charged by Odo to visit him. We are to find out as much as we can about his intentions. Then we must visit Edith and report back back at speed to Odo in Canterbury.'

'All these important people you know,' she said, with a sad smile. 'Will you always be at the beck and call of powerful men?' I left Medstead in a warm glow.

The next day, Lēofric let out a gasp when he saw Stigand in his cell.

'You have lost so much weight, my Lord uncle,' he said as he moved to the old man's side.

'Ah, my troublesome little Lēofric. Yes, I have lost much weight and a great deal more besides. Come, pull up a stool and hold my hand.'

He turned to me. 'And you', he said, 'must be Gilbert of Bayeux, the creature of the odious Odo. Should I let you hold my other hand, the one where my ring of office used to be?'

'My Lord bishop,' I replied offering another of my many bows. 'I am indeed a creature of my master and here at his bidding.'

Stigand coughed violently and the effort seemed to shake his whole body. 'At least a partly honest creature. Have you come to torture me?' His slight laugh sent him shaking again.

'What have they done to you, Uncle?'

'Not so much apart from starving me of company and of information from the world outside. They have placed me on this threadbare throne in order to mock me and here, look,' he held up his free arm, 'they have imprisoned me with this delicate silver chain and placed my books just too far to reach. I sit here in silence, unable to move to the gate. My guards do not come when I call, but wait until I soil myself. It has all brought me closer to God.'

'Have you received no visitors, Uncle, in all this time?'

'Another of Odo's creatures, Hugh de Port, also of dubious parentage, calls by twice a week, although I lose track of time, even day and night. He usually eats a fruit in front of me. Last time, he left me the apple core. I ignore him although he is persistent with his questions.

'I am sure I saw Odo peeping around the corner some weeks ago. I called to him, but he scuttled away. Now, he in contrast to me has put on weight. Then my usurper, Walkelin, came in once and denounced me in anger for my crimes. I fear Walkelin. Whatever I have done or not done, Walkelin is capable of much more. And last, just a week ago, my queen came finally to see me. She has chosen her side and forsaken me. May God curse the Godwinsons and all the great damage they have done to my country. Edith dared tell me that I should look after myself better. Such shaming irony.'

I asked Stigand if he thought he knew why Odo had sent us.

'William is terrified of a successful rebellion. He needs to know whether I will ever repeat Edward's deathbed words. Odo has been charged to find out. You are here as an innocent young man to find out how much I am a danger to William's conquered kingdom. Little Lēofric is here to make me drop my guard.'

Wizened and frail Stigand might be, but there was nothing wrong with his political skills.

'Now,' he said, 'I am tired. This is the most talking that I have done since I came to this foul place, except in my prayers. Come back tomorrow and by then I will have decided how much to share with you – and with Odo. Why not bring parchment and ink so that you do not have to trust to memory when you make your report? Please go now.'

Lēofric kissed his 'uncle' on the forehead while I used up another bow.

'Either he is going to tell us something useful to Odo or he will not,' decided Lēofric. 'Whatever, his idea of us writing down what he actually says is a good one. We will look efficient and loyal.'

We were back at the cell the next morning. There was little formality. Lēofric handed over a small sack with apples and pears and, on the top, some marzipan which Stigand sucked greedily. I set up a small table with a stool and placed parchment ready.

'Well, my Lord, have you decided?'

'I have. You must let me tell my own story in my own way without questions as if I was speaking to God.'

'You may well be doing just that, Stigand,' I said to myself. Stigand spoke in Latin, the tongue of the church.

I was always a strong supporter of Harold despite his many faults. When no more could be done for his cause, I submitted to William. Ealdred of York, Thomas's predecessor, anointed William at Westminster. I was present but, because I had been excommunicated many times, could not act which I would have done. So, in Thomas and I, York, Canterbury and Winchester were all represented. It was the same position when William's wife, Matilda, was crowned queen two years later. Would I have done this had I not accepted William as a king out of right?

William is an effective ruler and well-liked by his own kind. Whenever he goes out, he is seized upon by the crowds and nudged hither and thither and, surprising to say, listens to each man with patience, and, though assaulted by all with shouts and pullings and rough pushings, does not challenge anyone for it, nor show any appearance of anger.

He is not an appealing man. He is rigid, puritanical, corrupt, cruel and greedy. He is an outstanding soldier, a very capable general and a warrior who leads by example. He is possessed of great fortitude and acts with an unbending insistence on his own authority. He tries to keep peace within his lands, do justice firmly, punish savagely and to protect the Church. However, he is shameless and ruthless in his manipulation of facts to justify dubious enterprises.

I have been accused of acquiring wealth. I am guilty. I did so to protect my family. For me, personally, the trappings are valueless other than good wine and comfort. If I am guilty then so is William and all his barons and bishops. Greed and avarice disfigure their characters much more than mine. I placed my personal wealth at Ely Abbey for safekeeping, but it was taken by William along with my estates. William and his kind also took gold and silver from the people unjustly and with little need.

I was condemned on ecclesiastical charges, but these could have been made after the conquest or even before when papal legate Ermenfrid last visited England. William did nothing to protect me. Any good that I had done was of no matter. This all suggests that my removal was primarily political and part of the great plan to make England irredeemably Norman. Note that after my removal only foreigners are now chosen as bishops. There will be no more bishops from the old kingdom.

At my trial, I chose to keep my peace. I recognised the inevitability of all that was happening about and to me. Now with you, my new inquisitors, untainted men, unkindly sent, I will give some answers.

I was charged with three offences.

The first was plurality, that I kept against all papal instruction the sees of Canterbury and Winchester at the same time. If this is a crime, then, of course, I am guilty. But reflect that my predecessor at Canterbury, Robert de

Jumièges, was deposed and forced into exile because he dared to oppose the mighty earl Godwin by trying to regain lands that rightfully belonged to the church. The real reasons lay underneath. Robert had travelled to Normandy to tell duke William that Edward wanted him for his heir. This was something that the Godwinsons could not accept. Also damning was his proposal that Edward should divorce Edith which would eat at the Godwinsons' power. Robert was a saintly man, unfairly sacrificed. A strong man was required to resist that family's further encroaches and I did so by holding both sees. The Godwinsons had only one plan, similar to that of William, to rule and plunder the kingdom.

Second, it was argued that I took the pallium of Robert de Jumièges when he fled. Here again, I was guilty for all the reasons stated before.

Third, that I received my own pallium in Rome from Benedict, called an anti-pope. Guilty. However, my intransigency towards papal authority is no argument to describe the English church as backward and in need of reform. While in some part it is true, it is the papal authorities that need reform. This is what Benedict stood for and why his name has been dragged through the mud. The power of the victors in the struggle for control in the holy city has won the day and become the new orthodoxy.

The writers of history may well be unkind to me. So be it. To the conquerors, I say that you do not ponder contritely in your hearts that you conquered not by your own strength but by the will of almighty God and that you subdued a people that was greater, richer and older than you are. To the people, I commend the law imposed from Cnut that everyone should learn the Lord's Prayer and the Creed.

I have no more to say and will answer no questions.

Stigand blessed us both as we kissed his bare ring finger and left.

'Good God almighty,' offered Lēofric. 'Did you manage to keep pace and to write all that down?'

'I did, although it will all have to be redrafted. Some parts, I will have to alter. As it is, I think we will be in danger just for hearing Stigand's words. Having a copy in a safe place may be the best defence that we have.'

I thought it best to move quickly to Wilton to tie up any loose ends before sending a report to Odo. There was a definite change when we were both admitted to Edith's presence. It was nothing immediately serious, yet it was evident that her attention was beginning to waver. Her incisiveness was sometimes missing; she repeated a few words unnecessarily. It was not something I was used to and I found it difficult to handle. She came fully to life when I showed her some draft embroidery with her requested storyline at the beginning. I also discussed those people who were to be named or embroidered, but she lost interest as soon as the portrayal of herself, and her husband, and, surprisingly, Stigand were agreed. Even the representation of the slaughter of her brother, Harold, did not capture her as before. She readily agreed the inclusion of Saint Ailgifu which I skipped through and allowed her to assume it was a requirement of Odo. I made sure that her companion nuns would be able to substantiate the agreement. The one thing on which she remained adamant was that the embroidery would be brought to her at Wilton before it left for Bayeux.

Back at Winchester, I settled down with parchment and ink to write four documents to be taken by fast messenger to Canterbury. Lēofric sat opposite me and we discussed each phrase before I committed it to the pen. Even then, our first efforts were put to the fire.

It took a day and a half to construct Stigand's defence. It was not long, but it was dense. After much debate, several things he said were left out, in truth as much for our protection as for that of the old man. We then worked for half a day on our own copy and my explanatory letter to Odo so that he would be in no doubt that I was a faithful and diligent recordist. We had no part in the content. The words all belonged to Stigand. I concluded with a heartful promise of confidentiality. I lied and said that there was no copy.

Next day, Lēofric asked permission to go about some private business. Frankly, I was pleased to have a break from the intensity. He was not needed as I began to construct some rough drawings of the preparation for the conquest as I recalled it for abbot Scolland. I started with the influence of the comet. Odo was at Bayeux sitting beside William, taking charge, issuing instructions to his men to begin work on the fleet and its provisions. On the left of this group, I drew Hugh de Port taking an active and important part and, thereby, fulfilled my obligation to him. Then, I placed men at work chopping trees, building boats, pulling them to the water, loading arms, chainmail, helmets and much else, and, finally, horses and men.

Lēofric came back and approved my efforts and then could contain himself no longer.

'I have found a stitcher,' he announced. 'This woman is highly skilled at embroidery. She is confident that given a full day she can add the extra pieces that we need. I have agreed the price and said that if she keeps the secret, I will pay her double after a year. She is no lover of the Normans.'

He paused. 'Besides,' he offered with a grin, 'she is a widow who likes me. I think I might have to call on her again to go over the details before we do the work. Her name is Mildgyth, which means *hope*. I think that is appropriate.'

'As long as she doesn't let us down at the last minute because she is fed up with you. And keeps her mouth shut.'

The last document, also for Scolland, but also surely to be viewed by Odo was where to place the others we and Edith had agreed to name in the embroidery. It was quite brief although I did give some suggestions for two of the main participants, Edward and Harold and then William's coronation as an appropriate end. I reiterated Edith's required poses. I added two more suggestions for Odo: one feasting, a popular companion; the other swinging a mace on horseback at the battle to show his leadership and heroism. A mounted Wadard was placed leading a foraging party before the battle; Vital I suggested as a mounted knight with lance and shield being interrogated by William on the disposition of Harold's forces. For Scolland, I thought a discreet figure in the upper frieze above the early scenes with his hands outstretched showing he was a witness.

And, finally, for our subterfuge, I placed a robed Ailgifu, implicitly one of Harold's daughters, standing in a building that could have been a meeting place with her hands raised in submission. Above the doorway sat the heads of two cockatrices. Beside her stood her clerk. I requested a pig as one of the animals in the bottom frieze.

7 FUNERALS AND A WEDDING, 1072

The wedding ended on a sour and unexpected note even though the omens had been good. I wrote to Odo and Scolland that I was at their call, but that I hoped to be left free in January to attend to my marriage arrangements. They replied that my work was as expected and cursorily wished me well; no immediate meetings in Canterbury were needed. However, it soon seemed that, no matter where I was, the machinations of the king and his bishops would find me out and crash into my life.

Lēofric, carrying some of my silver pennies for Ailgifu's expenses, worked hard to make a success of the day. Having estimated likely attendees, enough food and drink arrived in a cart from Winchester to cater for twice that number. As a result, Medstead was lavishly supplied deep into a bleak February. Blessings arrived from Scolland and Stigand and gifts of jewellery, no doubt plunder, came from Hugh de Port in Winchester and Adam fitz Hubert at Dover Castle. Odo sent a fat purse which, I must admit, I thought was no more than my due. I put it aside, unused, to give to Ailgifu on our first morning as, I hoped, an unexpected *morgengifu*. It would assure her long-term independence whatever happened in this dangerous world.

Lēofric gave us his gift in a quiet moment. Its thoughtfulness brought tears. He had acquired from I never knew where a worn but almost complete copy of *Geoponika*, a work compiled a hundred years before at the behest of the Byzantine emperor Constantine. It was an anthology of classical agricultural texts from a millennium of Greek and Latin writing on subjects of practical use from diplomacy to siege warfare to farming. Ailgifu's delight when Lēofric pointed out the lengthy section on bees and hives was fulsome reward. Bizarrely, this valuable book was reckoned by all to be the first tome other than the bible ever seen in the hamlet. People queued in wonder to touch the cover and study inside pages and their drawings.

At the porch, cattle and pigs were brought to join the ceremony of promise and fertility. Inside, the small church was a ramshackle revelation, gladly embracing both Christian and pagan ritual, the walls decorated with candles and holly with bright red berries. On the wall at the side near the front, the carved face of man surrounded by oak, hawthorn and ivy leaves was cracked and worn smooth by constant stroking. The whole village, plus others unknown from Ropley, crammed inside. I counted sixty people most of whom claimed a new relationship with me. The drink was free flowing and the dancing immodest, almost insane, in its commitment. Everyone wore bizarre, decorated head coverings for a reason I never fathomed. Ailgifu and I retired early, but had to keep getting up to acknowledge an hour of appearances at our upstairs window while bawdy toasts were drunk below.

We were interrupted in bed mid-morning by a shaking Lēofric, tears coursing down his face.

'Stigand is dead,' he announced. 'They say he died of old age and imprisonment, but the truth is known. He was murdered, poisoned, at the direction of Hugh de Port under the eye of that damned bishop Walkelin. Odo's hand is all over this.' Ailgifu sat wide-eyed and bare breasted with Odo's purse in her lap.

I knew that Walkelin was capable. A few months before, even Winchester, a town of sudden disappearances, was shocked when Abbot Ealdred of Abingdon had died in the bishop's personal custody while accused of organising discontent.

Lēofric grasped me by the shoulders, rage and horror driving him, and shook me hard.

'You know why they killed him? It's because of what we wrote. It was his death notice. This is our fault. We are murderers, too.'

I got up, unfortunately naked, and gave him a long hug telling him the fault lay elsewhere. We were not responsible for the world into which we had been born. After a few minutes, Ailgifu suggested I got back into bed as she thought the cold air was having a detrimental effect. I decided we would all leave for Winchester later that day. No doubt Odo would be calling for us to ensure we had not wavered on hearing the news. Lēofric's blood relationship to Stigand would be seen as a potential problem.

We had scarce arrived at the city before the streets were ablaze with more news and speculation. William's second son, Richard, was dead in the New Forest while hunting with his father and brother, the red-faced William. At first, the death was caused by an arrow; next, he had been waylaid and assassinated by a band of Saxons still loyal to the Godwinsons. There was to be a rebellion. A panic began when word arrived at the same time that Edith was at Wilton surrounded by a gathering of survivors from the old West Saxon regime. Armed men were ordered to the streets, the town gates closed and the castle drawbridge raised. Emotions ran high. The truth became clear just in time to stop serious trouble. Richard had been galloping headlong after a renowned stag when his head hit a low-hanging bough. It was an accident, well-witnessed.

As always, when the famous die young and tragically, Richard was recalled as a man of exceptional promise. William's return to Winchester was a doleful affair to the slow beat of saddle drums. Everyone was summoned to the streets to pay homage and to show personal sorrow. William looked like a beaten man, head sunk, riding slouched and showing none of his customary pugnacious swagger. It was Ailgifu's first sight of her hated king.

The New Forest was William's creation; a vast pleasure ground for a conquering king in thrall to the chase. However, behind the splendour was a grim picture of forced depopulation and the destruction of churches and villages. A consensus grew: Richard's death was surely a sign of God's disapproval: a payback for the murders of archbishop Stigand and abbot Ealdred.

Richard with great ceremony and Stigand, at least with honour, were both buried at the Old Minster. Ailgifu and I attended the bishop's funeral, the church filled to overflowing and soldiers lining the route of the coffin. Lēofric was one of the pall bearers.

We were soon ordered to Canterbury. Ailgifu decided to stay at our home rather than go so quickly back to Medstead. St Michael's church, behind our building, was one of Winchester's fifty churches. Most were tiny and unimpressive, but all showed Christian resilience at grass roots. Services in these small rooms were preached in English with traditional homilies. Ailgifu had used St Michael's to introduce herself to the immediate neighbourhood and had made friends and become popular with the shopkeepers. Besides, she said, there were plenty of places to explore.

'That's not what it's about,' complained Lēofric as we rode away with our escort. 'She's going to spend your money changing the house while we're at Canterbury. I told her that if she messes with my rooms downstairs I will ask your permission to beat her. She was very rude to me.'

Odo was even more animated than usual. The most propertied man in England after the king with castles at Dover, Rochester, Deddington in Oxfordshire and Snettisham in Norfolk, and a house in London and numerous estates across the country, was not going to give ground against claims for unlawful acquisition no matter who was making them. The difficulty was that the six claims came from archbishop Lanfranc who was trying to re-establish his Christchurch Cathedral estates. Lanfranc badly needed the money for building work. His claim was that before Odo stole the estates from English lords, those lords had stolen them first. He had the proof.

Odo was so dismayed that he hardly bothered to check my feelings about Stigand's 'unfortunate death'. I couldn't get him to concentrate on Edith's embroidery and I was thrust at abbot Scolland. Everything was 'excellent, approved, get on with it'. I left Lēofric to deal with the details as I was dragged off to court.

The estate claims were to be investigated at a local shire hearing at Penenden Heath near Maidstone, a place notorious for the hanging and burning of witches. Because of the eminence of the protagonists, William had appointed Geoffrey de Montbray, bishop of Coutances, to represent him and to preside. Geoffrey, a man with a brutal military reputation, a hero of Hastings, had rebuilt his cathedral in the style of Jumièges, the old Westminster Abbey of Edward the Confessor, and of Durham. He then lined it with loot from southern Italy. Geoffrey and Odo were a pair of fighting, avaricious bishops and good friends.

Odo insisted I attend the hearing and to 'stay close' in case he needed me 'to do something'. Odo had a joint defendant, Hugh de Montfort, who had provided fifty ships and sixty knights for the invasion and had been rewarded by country-wide estates and the castle at Winchester. I had not met Hugh and, because of his power in my home city, was not anxious to upset him. Odo introduced us and Hugh recognised my name. He looked a devious lizard and fixed me with his reptilian eyes. If he had a tail, I would not be surprised.

'Yes, Gilbert of Bayeux, I know the name. You have had dealings with my sheriff, Hugh de Port.'

The hearing was set to last three days; it seemed all the Frenchmen in the county were present. Odo and Hugh defended themselves, but their arrogance and lack of preparation got in the way of their arguments. Lanfranc, by contrast, had painstakingly researched the ancient rights and, as a result, Odo and Hugh were being thoroughly vanquished by the lawyer-monk. Odo pulled me to one side at the end of the second day and instructed me to talk to Lanfranc to see if a deal could be made. By good fortune, I thought, he agreed to see me that evening, but I should have realised there would be a second agenda. After some skirmishing, Lanfranc suggested he would make no more claims against Odo, which he said he could do, if Odo and Hugh would withdraw and return the cathedral lands. Lanfranc was prepared to fight on in public, but in private he was tired of the slow, hard bargaining.

'Every day, I endure so many troubles and vexations,' he said, as, slumped in a small throne, he ate a solitary late meal of bread, cheese and wine. 'I suffer such injury and distress, hardness of heart, greed and dishonesty.'

After a glass, he perked up. 'The model for Winchester Cathedral will come from the Abbaye-aux-Hommes at Caen,' he announced. 'Winchester is one of a number of new cathedrals I offered to placate the pope after William's unlawful marriage to Matilda.

'I want this new cathedral to show the clarity and order of the Norman church. Christ himself should be the treasure of the church and not some local cults worshipping bones kept in little village churches.'

The fervour increased as he spread his arms. 'I want Winchester to be a triumph of stone masonry. Its length will be unequalled by any other ecclesiastical building in western Christendom north of the Alps apart from St Hugh's great church in Cluny. There will be hundreds of worshippers in each congregation. Its huge basilica will proclaim the power of one faith under one church and one liturgy.'

His voice softened and he turned to me with a demon light burning in his eyes.

'Now, Gilbert, what I want from you is to help me build my new cathedral at Winchester. The designers, the masons and the craftsmen I will bring from here in Canterbury and from Christian cities overseas. What I need is a man I can trust to guard my purse and to bring together the materials on time and at the right price ready for when work starts in a year or so. Will you do this, do good work for God and also enjoy my bounty and protection?'

Those last points held serious attraction.

I put the deal to Odo. At first he was angry. I pointed out that, in my opinion and in that of most of the courtroom, he was going to lose. What he had to do was lose to his advantage. He could advance his reputation by saying that he had listened carefully to Lanfranc's arguments and found them persuasive. He would yield to save the time of the court and out of respect for the archbishop. In return, privately, he would know there would be no more pursuit from Lanfranc. There was one other price. Lanfranc wanted me to help him build his next cathedral at Winchester.

Odo walked slowly around the abbey cloister with me trailing. It took him five minutes to make his decision.

'Always you end up smelling of roses, Gilbert. You are an unusual man. I dislike what you have said, but I realise that you are right. This is an arrangement I can live with. Let Lanfranc know. I will graciously withdraw tomorrow. You obviously want the job with the cathedral. Well, I agree, as long as you have finished with the embroidery. I will call you again if I need something new and I will expect you to come running.'

He stopped walking and faced me.

'Is Lēofric under control?' It was the first time he had ever used his name.

'Yes, my Lord. Even now, busy at your work.'

'I always reward my faithful servants,' he said. 'What is your desire? You have not asked for a manor and some important title.'

'I seek a quiet life, Lord, with my new wife. What I would like as a gift for her is the freeholding of a few fields in Ropley. It is where she keeps the hives that make the borage honey that is now so popular with our noble king. I should also like a good purse for my man Lēofric. He is interested in a widow he has just met. He has been invaluable to your interests since introduced by Hugh de Port.'

'Unusual again, Gilbert. You ask for nothing directly for yourself. You shall have your two requests. Make us all proud of Winchester cathedral. And, now, I must explain to Hugh de Montfort that he has to give way to Lanfranc, too, tomorrow.'

The next afternoon, back at the abbey, I shared my adventure with Lēofric. He was almost as unhappy as Odo had been.

'You have done a deal with the murderer of my uncle,' he accused.

'You're right, Lēofric. I have dealt with the devil, but I have done it for our new church in Winchester, for Ailgifu and for you. It also gives us both good employment and more protection.'

I handed him Odo's clinking purse. 'This is for you. If you see it as blood money, then either make a donation that will do Stigand honour or feather the bed of your widow.' Leofric took the money and it was never mentioned again.

Leofric then took me to the well-advanced embroidery where eighteen stitchers were at work all chattering, in pairs, as their hands each moved several needles with highly-coloured threads deftly through nine pieces of linen. Even being so close to the embroidery's development, I was astounded at its quality and vibrancy. The most striking and recurring feature was the groups of knights in chainmail equipped with long shields and lances charging on their warhorses.

'Look,' said Leofric, 'look at the horrible lower border where the dead are depicted in terrible postures. They are lying amid a litter of abandoned shields, broken swords and wounded horses. I've done some counting. In all, there are about 600 people, 500 animals of all kinds, 200 horses and fifty trees.

'And here is Ailgifu already entered with you next to her. All that needs to be added is your extended arm. And here, below, in this gap is where I will be,' he giggled, 'passing my opinion on the Normans and their invasion.'

Leofric then took me to see Scolland. He had an new favour to ask of me, an instruction really.

'I understand that your customary path to Winchester takes you through Alton and then through the pass in the forest?' he asked. 'Then you must travel close to the village of Bentworth. It is part of the royal estate at Odiham. I have been there once to visit the great hall that is held by bishop Geoffrey for the king.'

Scolland explained that Geoffrey would leave Penenden Heath for Winchester. He was to attend a king's church council which would hear the now fractious dispute between Lanfranc and archbishop Thomas of York over the primacy of Canterbury over all England. Geoffrey would then embark on a long tour of several of his larger English estates, thought altogether to be about 280 manors, many in Somerset.

'What Geoffrey has asked,' continued Scolland, 'and Odo has agreed, is that he has a private viewing of the embroidery before it is seen by Edith and leaves for Bayeux. Geoffrey will be at Bentworth at the end of June. The work will be finished by then and packed in its special chest. You are to lead an armed guard from Canterbury to Bentworth to Wilton and from thence to Southampton. The king will first see the embroidery when it is displayed in the cathedral at Bayeux.'

He looked at me quizzically, unused to giving me orders. I nodded.

'Good. I'll leave you to work out the details. I'll tell Odo that all is settled.'

Lēofric and I returned to Winchester to find a different house. Workmen were on the roof repairing some wood tiles. A drainpipe, damaged by a cart, had been replaced. Holes in the wall where laths showed through, inside and out, had been filled and covered with white plaster. Both bedsteads were now placed in curtained alcoves for more privacy. New coloured rugs came from a maker one street away and, on them, some oak chests placed for clothes and linen with one kept especially for Ailgifu's kirtles, always blue with decorated hems. Our chess board was openly displayed on its own table, pieces ready to continue our battle. There was an additional carved and painted bench by a sturdy oak eating table. Two wall hangings that I thought I recognised from rooms at the library appeared after the next night. The soil pit in the garden was connected by sewer to an open drain in the churchyard and some men employed for monthly cleaning visits. Ailgifu had sent for some of her favourite pots, pans and drinking horns from Medstead and added large ewers for mead and water. There were even some snowdrops in rough black Saxon clay pots, one placed centrally in Lēofric's open space. His bed linen had been washed.

A few days later Mildgyth came to visit Ailgifu and they talked in the garden for a hour. The next morning a handcart arrived with her clothes and furniture and she moved in downstairs with Lēofric. There was a new regime in place with Mildgyth washing everyone's clothes every Friday and darning any holes in tunics, hose and skirts. I learned one of those useful lessons in life. If someone is a competent manager, you let them do their tasks in their own way leaving only compliments in your wake.

I bought Ailgifu a five-year-old mare which she stabled with *Thor* who was having a lengthy rest. She rode to Medstead once a week to inspect her hives and shop and to check up on her brothers. She often went with Mildgyth and stayed the night. One bright spring morning, a bishop's messenger arrived bringing papers from Odo. He had held his side of the bargain. I was the freehold tenant of three fields in Ropley sited on the left of the track before it climbed the chalk hill to the pond near Kitwood. The road was set deep into the slope where iron wheels and the tracks of cattle making for water had worn away the soft ground. Ailgifu's gratitude lasted a whole intense morning. It was no surprise at all when a man arrived from Alresford to show me plans for the house he had been instructed to build near the hives at Ropley.

Visits to Scolland became infrequent. In truth, we were not needed as the embroidery grew in length and decoration. This was the time of making, not a debate. I spent most of my hours in Canterbury with Lanfranc or, more particularly, with a senior mason. Sketches for the new cathedral with lists of requirements and tasks demanded two new chests of their own. I often paced the ground around Winchester's two main minsters debating with myself over schedules and sizes.

These days were some of the best in my life. I delighted in Ailgifu's company, her enthusiasm, her innocence and her willingness to learn.

Edith's condition deteriorated. She became impatient to see her great work even though she knew it would not arrive until June. On one trip, I took Ailgifu with me to see Sarum and its near-finished castle with its armoury and then to visit Wilton. In the background, the cathedral was growing within the fortified hilltop. Unusually empty of holy relics, the construction was portrayed as a City of God on Earth, with those close to heaven within and the devil's own without.

Wilton was a place that had lost its status, stripped in favour of Sarum, or Seorebryg, as Wiltshire's main town; its mint moved as well. The duties of the county sheriff were now undertaken by the castellan. At the abbey, Edith asked if I had come alone and then demanded to meet my wife. Ailgifu was dumbstruck to be invited into the royal presence, the queen of the famed king Edward. She kept her marzipan as a keepsake to show all she met.

In the third week of June, I led a troop of five men-at-arms to St Augustine's Abbey. Abbot Scolland was almost beside himself with excitement. He took me to the carefully folded embroidery with interleaved thin, waxed linen sheets. I opened a few leaves, announced myself stunned at the quality and management of the work. It took four men to lift it gently into its purpose-built chest. Scolland even added a hammer and a box of strong, narrow nails to be placed just a handsbreadth apart to carry the hanging.

'Odo loves it,' Scolland almost shouted. 'Everyone is in awe. I am in awe. You must take great care. Hang it carefully. Only set sail when the sea is flat calm.' He embraced me, kissed me on both cheeks, blessed the chest, blessed me and insisted on a prayer of some length.

Three days later our party with its cart and precious cargo arrived at Bentworth. The journey had been without incident. I carefully wiped down the chest after we waited under trees during one brief fall of rain. My heart lurched at every jolt from the numerous ruts in the road. I thought everyone who stopped work to stare at us when we passed believed we must be carrying the king's treasure. Would some consider an armed robbery?

Arriving at Alton, the dangerous forest was skirted to the north. We were eagerly expected, but bishop Geoffrey had not yet arrived. He had sent word ahead that he was two days' journey away. It was perfect timing. I sent two of my men to Medstead where my family of three were waiting, Mildgyth with a large cloth roll containing the tools of her trade. Her collection of wool threads from Winchester matched exactly those despatched to Scolland and his team of stitchers at the abbey.

Hall Place was a large two-storey wooden building about a mile from the church. It was surrounded by fences and a continuous ditch and recently built to Geoffrey's personal directions. The main entrance with its rounded arch was of stone imported from Caen. On its left stood an attached chapel for private worship. The block entered from the doorway contained meeting rooms with extensive kitchens, a buttery and storehouses behind with associated stables and privies all connected by wooden walkways. The multiple sleeping rooms and the bishop's private bower were upstairs. To the right, there was no second storey, but a large hall with open oak beams in a high roof which gave the building its name. It was designed to act as the public part of the complex where manorial dues and and services were rendered and as a hunting lodge for royal parties. The hall was filled with trestles for feasts for large numbers of visitors. The chest was laid carefully on a central table. I measured around the room. Big as the hall was, it was no match for the nave at Odo's new cathedral at Bayeux. The embroidery would need to stretch almost twice around covering the door once. Those who came to gawp would have to bend at the door to slip underneath when it was hung.

When my fellow conspirators arrived, the women bursting with excitement and Lēofric hardly less so, I suggested we first unwrapped a few layers so that the admiration would not impede the hanging. Ailgifu thought it a miracle made in heaven. Mildgyth just stood, jaw dropped, fists clenched and breathing heavily.

We started to hang the embroidery. Lēofric banged in the nails and we unwrapped and shifted a trestle until all was complete. It took four hours. Standing back, I could not believe its cumulative effect. I accepted finally that we had been part of something truly special and a wonder of the Christian world.

I then explained to Ailgifu what we had secretly done and took her to the panel where her name and robed figure appeared at the doorway of Wherwell Abbey. The cockatrice heads at the tops of its columns were the same as the one above the door at her mead shop.

'We have written the name as *Ælgyva* so that no one will doubt that this lady is English,' I explained.

I thought she would faint in fear of sacrilege. I then showed her the Norman figure standing to the right, explaining that it was me and the writing above said that I was her *clericus*. In the next panel after a church, duke William directed armed men.

'The first thing that you must do,' I said to Mildgyth, 'is to extend my arm, here, so that my fingers are touching erotically the chin of this beautiful woman. It will suggest that we have a deep relationship and are in love. The woman's hands are both raised in the accepted gesture of sexual agreement. No one will fully understand who these people are, but we will know. Each party believes that the instruction for this small part of the tableaux was given by another. It has no provenance.

'Then, by long agreement, we must include my friend Lēofric. Like you, he hates the Norman invaders. He wants to take some small revenge for what he knows to be the murder of his uncle, the bishop Stigand. He also hates that this work,' and I threw out my arm to encompass the whole room, 'is being used as false justification for William's invasion.'

'What are you going to do?' gasped Ailgifu. 'Even if it is an unholy witness, it is still magnificent. It cannot be harmed.'

'What Mildgyth is going to do,' said Lēofric, 'is to place my unnamed figure here in this section of the lower frieze beneath one of the pillars of your shop, sorry, shrine. There is a pig there at the moment. I shall be naked. I shall be holding my right arm up in an unseemly sign toward Gilbert. I shall be squatting and I shall be shitting on the whole Norman artifice.'

There was a long moment of silence and then the laughter started and we all hugged each other until tears fell down our cheeks.

'I shall have to draw you with a very large phallus,' said Mildgyth, most seriously. 'I insist that people will be able to recognise that it is you.'

And the laughter started all over again. It was some while before Mildgyth began work. She sewed carefully and calmly through the night so that she and Ailgifu could be well gone by the time Geoffrey arrived.

I think it was the next day while waiting for the bishop that I realised for the first time that I was no longer Norman, but decidedly English, whatever that might mean.

Four bishops

Stigand, archbishop of Canterbury, bishop of Winchester, appointed 1052-1070

Walkelin, bishop of Winchester, appointed 1070-1098

Lanfranc, archbishop of Canterbury, appointed 1070-1089

The seal of Anselm, archbishop of Canterbury, appointed 1093-1109

Four kings

Harold Godwinson, reigned 1066-1066

William the Conqueror, reigned 1066-1087

William Rufus, third son of the conqueror, reigned 1087-1100

Henry Beauclerc, fourth son of the conqueror, reigned 1100-1135

Four aspirants

Robert Curthose, duke of Normandy, first son of the conqueror, born c. 1051-1134

Odo, earl of Kent and bishop of Bayeux, born c. 1035-1097

Ranulf Flambard, bishop of Durham, born c. 1060-1128, escaping from the Tower of London

Eustace II, count of Boulogne (Eustace aux Grenons, long moustaches), c. 1015-c. 1087, lord of the manor of Sutton (including Ropley) and father of Baldwin I, king of Jerusalem, elected 1100-1118. Above him flies the comet

From the Bayeux Tapestry

Ailgifu beneath the Wherwell cockatrices is touched on her face by the loving hand of Gilbert, her *clericus*. Below, the arm of Lēofric reaches upwards

Lēofric squats in the lower frieze showing his displeasure, one arm reaching upwards towards Ailgifu and Gilbert

113

Abbot Scolland, a discreet figure in the upper frieze above the early scenes with his hands outstretched showing he was a witness

Alresford's forged charter

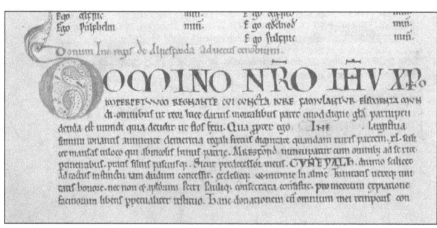

The beginning of the grant of king Ine to Winchester Cathedral of land at Alresford, A.D. 701, with the name of Ine scratched in

8 ALMOST EVERYTHING TO RUBBLE, 1073-1082

What followed the delivery of the embroidery was a bit of a let down. My two showings passed almost without incident. Bishop Geoffrey was not in the best of moods when he turned up a day late after dealing with some recalcitrant tenants. He spent two hours working his way along the tableaux from Edward's death to William's coronation. His humour was not improved when he realised his role at Hastings was not recognised. I advised him to mention this to his great friend Odo as I was under strict instruction not to agree any changes and, anyway, did not have the capability. There was still plenty of time and space to add his name above one of the gallant horsemen. I suspected that this was just the beginning of aggrieved requests and did not want any disappointment to fall on my shoulders.

Edith almost fell on the chest when we arrived at Wilton. At her instruction, we placed the embroidery on a refectory table. We were not allowed to hang it which was a relief. Then, we were ushered from the room and told not to come back for two days. I do not know what changes she made. I was sure there were some. Nothing was ever mentioned by her or anyone else.

The delay worked in my favour because the night before my departure for the coast, Hugh de Port turned up with a guard party. He was returning to Bayeux on family business and when he suggested to Odo that he escort the embroidery to the cathedral, his offer was accepted and I was excused. I was pleased. I would rather return to Ailgifu than travel to Normandy. What it did mean was that neither Lēofric nor I ever saw the great addition to the glory of Odo's new church in its intended place. I did hear that Bayeux became a suitably splendid building with monumental carvings to match Odo's extravagant tastes. The embroidery attracted many visitors, but we didn't hear how well it fitted the nave. We never saw it again.

Ailgifu wanted to celebrate my early return with a meal of my choosing. She made it plain to Lēofric that this was to be a private affair and he was welcome to go out with Mildgyth for the evening. As we wandered through the market, enjoying the bustle and barter of the early evening, I chose some ribs of pig. For some reason, I thought of Lēofric's story of the linguistic conflict between *stōl* and *chaise* which I shared with Ailgifu.

'I was just thinking,' I said, 'that you use your words for animals for their meat as well, words, like pig, cow, calf, sheep. With the Normans, they often name their animals by the cooked meat, like *porc, boeuf, veau, mouton.*'

'That's easy,' offered Ailgifu. 'We English look after our animals. We see them being born, pasture them and kill them for food and clothing. The first time a Norman noble sees an animal, apart from a horse or a dog, is when they put them in their mouth. These French words will never catch on. They are words of the invaders.'

We were sitting outside close together on a bench with comfortable cushions, feet tucked near to a small log fire. The house was empty as Lēofric had taken Ailgifu's advice. The churchyard was quiet and our home blocked much of the noise from the street. I had skewered the ribs and dribbled mead on them for flavour and turned them regularly to keep them from burning. We were discussing our unloved king who had left for Normandy after the death of his son, Richard, and hadn't been seen in Winchester since. He was apparently caught up in multiple skirmishes in his troublesome dukedom. Lēofric had reported that William abandoned trying to learn the language of his wicked subjects. He also felt empowered to increase the rapacity of taxation. He felt less and less sympathy or empathy with his acquired kingdom. I wondered, now that Lanfranc was regent and I was working for him, whether my prospects would improve.

There was a strong scent on the early summer air which I knew well from the kitchens at Bayeux. Earlier, I had traced it to a hidden bush of rosemary. I learned that this plant was now scarce around Winchester after being left behind and forgotten after the Roman occupation. When the pork was just ready and on its platter, I stripped a handful of leaves and rubbed them in.

'You're full of surprises,' Ailgifu said. 'This tastes really good.' She ate steadily placing the meat so the fat would drain onto bread. 'I love crispy pig skin.' Then she said, 'I have a surprise for you, too. Would you like a boy or a girl?'

We went to bed soon after. Ailgifu assured me that the baby was at least six months' away and wouldn't be at all bothered today by my earnest attentions.

The news of yet another attempted rebellion almost passed us by. It was an odd affair, reported to me by acquaintances at the castle. The king, absent abroad, refused permission for Breton Ralph de Gael, earl of East Anglia, to marry Emma, the daughter of the first earl of Hereford. They went ahead anyway and treason was plotted at the wedding feast. As a consequence, the two earls rose in an undistinguished revolt.

To be honest, I didn't pay much attention. I heard that one of the earls, Roger de Breteuil of Hereford, was stopped at the River Severn by the Worcestershire militia. The fate of the second earl, Ralph, the over enthusiastic husband, was more directly interesting to me. He met a superior force at Cambridge led by the two bishops, Odo and Geoffrey de Montbray, Bentworth's infrequent visitor, and fled to Norwich. Leaving Emma, his wife, to defend the castle, Roger hotfooted to Denmark and returned with a fleet of 200 ships under Cnut. The expedition came to nothing and the newly-weds lost their English estates retiring to Emma's lands in Brittany. Bishop Geoffrey, true to form, promised to cut off the right foot of all captured rebels. Odo, no doubt, agreed.

The part played by Waltheof, the first earl of Northumbria, in the uprising was always in dispute. Some thought him deeply implicated. Others thought he was sworn to secrecy by a drunken oath when he overheard details of the plot. Whatever, Waltheof got cold feet and confessed his knowledge to archbishop Lanfranc. Lanfranc wrote to William in Normandy advising him that there was a revolt, but that it was under control. There was no need for him to return to England. Lanfranc also sent a monk who acted as an emissary to discuss the matter with the king and to report back.

However, Waltheof decided to visit William to beg forgiveness. This was Waltheof's second rebellion and, apparently, William's patience snapped. William brought the earl back to England and imprisonment in Winchester even though the court would not confirm his guilt or innocence.

'At least William has his last English earl under his control,' Lēofric commented. 'But, of course, he has to to keep his myth of legitimacy alive.'

A week before Christmas, my daughter arrived, healthy and noisy. A few days later, we heard that queen Edith had died. I had had no contact with her since our meeting with the embroidery. She and Stigand were declining memories and, in a way, I was pleased. It was time for a quieter life preparing for the new cathedral. Edith had been buried at Westminster next to her husband with all the honours of a high-born royal lady. I was happy, however, that at the end there seemed no bitterness. Although Lēofric, being Lēofric, did suggest that William would be determined not to let her lie at Wilton with the possibility of a cult growing around her tomb.

It seemed natural for us to call the new baby Edith.

Shortly afterwards trouble began with the plans for the new cathedral. A variety of stone was to be used including Quarr limestone from the Isle of Wight, Bath stone, Caen stone from Normandy, ashlar, Beer stone and Purbeck Marble. One of my tasks was to decide the amount of stone which could be reused from the two existing minsters when they were demolished. The New Minster had a small crypt at one end and I was down below with candles and workmen finishing this assessment when I noticed the dampness of the stone which had been quarried from Portland about 150 years before. In places, it was so bad that it fell away at the pressure of a dagger.

The intended site of the new cathedral to the south of where I stood was already specified. William gave lands in Alton and Clere in exchange for the cemetery of the New Minster so that planning could start and it could be cleared of bodies. My worry was that the crypt of the great new cathedral would be much deeper, as indeed, would be the stonework to take the great weight of a soaring nave and a dominating spire. I ordered my men to where the new tower would stand and ordered them to dig a large hole in the clay to the estimated depth of the foundations. At the height of a man, the shovels hit a Roman floor of thin red brick. The next day we trebled the depth and by mid afternoon found we were digging in peat. We returned on the third day to go further only to discover our large hole was one third full of brown water. Frogs were already at play. It seems that by breaking through the top peat layer, trapped water had been encouraged to escape upwards. In any event, how would peat be strong enough to hold up a stone cathedral?

I was due a visit in a month from the master mason at Canterbury. I had always found life-long masons to be placid, patient if determined individuals. It went with the territory. Perhaps it was the pressure from Lanfranc. On the one hand he was rebuilding his fire-damaged national icon while on the other enthusing and pushing his national minster building programme. Whatever it was, it had made Master Mason Landy into a miserable, testy, stick-in-the-mud. Disliking him was immediately a pleasure. I showed him first my calculations and he made some corrections and then insisted on the importation of more Caen stone when it would only be hidden by cladding or plaster. I made the mistake of pointing this out and did a rough calculation showing an increase in overall cost of a tenth.

Master Landy's head came to my shoulders. His face was ruddy with years of outdoor work and framed by unfashionable, unkempt long hair. His temper was probably chipped away by constant management of lacklustre, casual workers. He spat on the ground, looked up at me and asked me how many cathedrals I had built.

I handled the situation badly, of course. I, too, spat on the ground and then gave a pretence of deep thought.

'About none, Master Landy,' I replied, 'as you well know. But then I do know about money and how to look after my Lord archbishop's budgets.'

'Just do what you're told and you might keep your inflated job,' he ordered.

'All right, Master Landy. Thank you for listening. I'll make plain your requirements. There is just one other important item that we should discuss.'

I took him to my water-filled hole.

'So!' he demanded.

'This is where the tower of our cathedral is meant to be. I thought you would like to know that you will be building on water-logged peat.'

He was enraged.

'I've told you not to pretend this is your cathedral. If there are any problems, I will deal with them. This is where the king and the archbishop have decided that the cathedral is going to be.' His final gesture was to spit into the middle of the water causing a frog to leap out of the way.

I went home and spent two days writing my report to Lanfranc with detailed costs and timings from when permission was given to start. I identified the various major suppliers, all of whom had been contacted. I pointed out Master Landy's request for more Caen stone which would be concealed. I drew a map of the water pit and pointed out both my lack of expertise and my concern for the building's integrity. For good measure, I listed the fourteen major saints and kings that would need to be moved somewhere when the minsters were demolished. If they were to go to the new cathedral, their new resting places would be cramped and would need to be planned.

A month later, I received a note from Lanfranc's senior clerk thanking me on behalf of the archbishop for my excellent work and offering a very satisfactory payment. There was no comment about Landy's request for more Caen stone, nor about the watery peat. My involvement was at an end and I complained no more. I had a few small projects to undertake for Odo. It promised to be an easy summer when I could spend time with my special daughter. After all, as everyone agreed, building wasn't my subject.

I was sitting in the garden with Edith asleep on my legs. I was admiring her squat nose, white cheeks and small curls when a king's messenger arrived. Ailgifu was waiting for the first sign of waking so that she could begin a feed. Her breasts were heavy with milk. The messenger was not from the king who was, as usual, in Normandy. Instead, I was summoned to Hugh de Montfort's chamber at noon. Lēofric was to accompany me.

'Have you been a bad clerk?' suggested Ailgifu. 'Perhaps you are to be fined for building a watering hole on the bishop's grass? Maybe you have been selected to lead an invasion of Normandy?'

'As the call is from Hugh de Montfort, I can guarantee the task will not be pleasant,' I countered. 'I sense that my instant dislike of him was only matched by his of me.'

Even readied for bad news, no number of guesses, however wild, could have dreamed the horror that had been selected for the two of us. Much of what was done in the name of God and king in Norman England was disquieting or disgusting and, of course, some people revelled in it, sought out participation or delighted in the pain of others. Preoccupation with the prescribed religious framework under which we lived explained why there was profound indifference to the circumstances of people's deaths. The main concern, the constant debate, was the fate of someone's soul.

The soul under discussion was that of the cursorily noticed Waltheof, earl of Northumbria, currently languishing in a far from dry cell somewhere well below Montfort's castle chamber. Lēofric had a continuing interest in Waltheof's progress as the last of the pre-conquest English earls. All others were now Norman. Waltheof was the child of Scandinavian and Saxon nobility and his father, at one time, was the regent of almost all northern England.

'He's always been devout and charitable,' said Lēofric. 'He has spent his months of captivity in prayer and fasting. He wants to go to a monastery. Most people think he's not guilty as he repented before anything was done. Significant isn't it, that the two Norman earls who did fight are not held in Winchester.

One's getting fat in Brittany; the one called Roger from Hereford was also tried for treason before the Great Council, but was sentenced to life imprisonment.

'And do not forget that Waltheof is married to Judith de Lens, William's niece.'

Montfort was at his most pompous and curt. We joined eight citizens of Winchester. Those I knew were prominent in their own work, but all on the outside edge of the inner circle of power. Waltheof, the supposed English traitor, had been found guilty of rebellion against the king. He was to be beheaded tomorrow morning on St Giles Hill and we gentlemen were to be his escort and to witness the just deed. We would meet at dawn at the castle's west entrance to follow the condemned man. There would be no excuses or exceptions. The executioner and our party would be accompanied by mounted, armed men.

I sensed Lēofric tense and grabbed an arm in a painful squeeze before he risked his life by an impassioned outburst.

No one except my Edith slept that night. I intended to keep the news from Ailgifu but, in the small hours, worn down by her demands to know what was happening, my resolve broke. I finally snatched a few hours' sleep in her arms with Edith by our side.

Just as the sun broke over the castle, the party began its slow descent of the High Street, the light gradually showing our path. I saw no dignitaries. Waltheof was on his knees in straw at the back of a simple cart. A masked man sat above him holding the reins loosely with a vicious curved axe propped in a corner. Although no public notice had been given, the road filled with murmuring English watchers of all ranks. The sun rose quickly, weakening the early mist and giving the procession an ethereal feel. Long shadows fell on the downward slope. This was no slow walk to hope, but to despair. The air was filled with sullen anger with no hint of celebration. I felt that if the banner of Wessex was raised, Lēofric would have led the patriotic charge to free the earl and storm the castle. After East Gate was passed, opened early, we began to climb the steep rise to where a block was already in place.

The execution was an embarrassment to everyone, not that one can criticise a condemned man for begging for more time. Waltheof was allowed to kneel and to say the *Lord's Prayer*, but he kept pausing as if to put off his end. The executioner lost patience and cut off his head in one stroke before the last words were said.

I was forced to stand near by, so close to have some fear of the swinging axe. My tunic and hose were spattered with blood spurting from the open neck. I saw the head fall to the ground and roll twice before stopping face upwards. I never saw what others swore afterwards they saw. Waltheof's lips moved and in a thin voice, as from another world, completed the prayer with *Libera nos a malo*.

As the group slowly made its way back down the hill, some soldiers threw the body into a ditch and the executioner kicked the head after it. Lēofric and I stayed a while and, when the guards had gone, found some turfs and covered the corpse.

The miracle of the prayer was soon the talk of the city. Waltheof in death had proved his innocence beyond doubt. He was canonised by the longings of an afflicted population. The downtrodden comforted themselves with two mythical hero-saints, the unsteady Waltheof and Edward, the lover of Normans. Among the oppressed, imagination tried to address the facts. Misfortunes to be suffered later in William's reign would clearly result from the truth of Waltheof's sanctity.

I was more shaken by the beheading that I cared to admit. If you are not a soldier, not hardened to the wounds that ripped bodies to the bone so that entrails and brain lay all around in bloody gore, the sight of a gushing neck can do more than wrench your stomach. I turned thirty and lost the youthful spirit that ignores any hint of one's own vulnerability, one's own death. Over the next few years, I grew fearful for Ailgifu and Edith, in fact everyone I cared for.

One day in 1079, I started a stroll, a regular pleasantry, around the minsters with my family of five, yes, we had been joined in turn by Emma and Andrew, Jesus's first disciple. All were healthy, thank God, and Ailgifu grew prettier to me with every birth. I heard a shout and saw Master Mason Landy striding towards me. I was recognised and remembered without animosity. Considering the way I had thought of him over the last few years, I was a little humbled. He grabbed my arm and took me to my old pit which was now ten times its previous size. After some dry months, the bottom was a little muddy but otherwise there was no water. Landy was excited.

'See, it has dried out,' he explained. Work had finally started on the cathedral foundations. 'We are going to lay a giant raft of logs two deep on which to build, all held in place by other trunks driven deep into the ground. The peat is a man's depth, but underneath there is river gravel which carries water from the

Itchen. Our raft will be as strong and firm as a herd of oxen and will last at least a thousand years.'

I wondered what would happen when the peat compressed with the weight of a church of God or the wood finally rotted, but, a wiser man, I kept my counsel.

'That's a lot of wood,' I ventured.

'It's a funny story,' he offered. 'Do you know of Hempage Forest?'

I did. The forest was a beautiful wooded place at Avington, a short distance before Alresford. I passed it regularly on my rides to Medstead.

'And you know that, now we have started to build, responsibility has passed from Lanfranc in Canterbury to Walkelin here in Winchester?'

This was certainly new to me, but it made complete sense. Landy told me his story while Ailgifu sat on the grass and played with the children.

Walkelin accepted that he needed to shore his new cathedral from the peat and water. William gave him no choice but to build on the minster site. In return, Walkelin asked the king, the owner of all woodlands, for a source of oak and beech to build his raft as well as for the cathedral floors and ceilings. The king offered Hempage Wood, but only where it was thick and deer could not pass through and, specifically, only what could be taken in three days.

The archbishop collected a large troop of carpenters by scouring the city and all the local villages. Within the three days, the whole wood was cut down and carried to Winchester.

'Just one mature tree was left standing,' gasped Landy, still excited by the act. 'It was the Gospel Oak where they used to beat the manor boundary and read the gospel because St Augustine once preached there, the man who brought Christianity to England and established Canterbury as its centre.'

Soon afterwards, the king passed by Hempage and, struck with amazement, cried out, 'Am I bewitched or have I taken leave of my senses? Had I not once a most delectable wood upon this spot?' When William understood what had happened, he was enraged.

'Walkelin was forced to put on a shabby vestment,' exclaimed Landy. 'He crawled to the king's feet and begged humbly to resign as bishop. He asked that he might retain his royal friendship and chaplaincy for he was the king's cousin.'

'Good heavens,' was about all I could manage. 'What happened next?'

'The king gave way saying that he was as much too liberal in his grant as Walkelin was too greedy in taking advantage of it.'

'So, Walkelin lives on in Winchester free from threat?'

'He does and I now have a cathedral to build on a raft of Hempage wood.'

Landy explained that skilled itinerant masons had arrived from castles and cathedrals nearing completion in Normandy, France, Germany, Italy and the north of England. Professional stone carvers for the gargoyles and interior work would follow them. The first masons from Milan were already housed in temporary accommodation near the Nunnaminster.

'I was surprised how easy local unskilled labour was to find,' he said. 'We pay better than field rates without the seasonal hunger. They do most of the first phase carving and shaping which needs muscles not brains. If they learn well they have a job for life. We Normans are always building something.'

My walks with Ailgifu became family highlights. I enjoyed them hugely for the opportunities to play with the children as they too quickly grew. Once, Ailgifu decided that we should climb St Giles Hill to try to exorcise my ghosts. Waltheof had been exhumed after a few years and given a more fitting burial in Winchester. The story was, of course, that his body was uncorrupted. The abbot at Crowland Abbey near Peterborough, part built by Waltheof, sought the king's permission to 'remove his bones and to bury him with much honour'. When the tomb was opened, the head had miraculously been reattached. More miracles followed near the tomb and a great deal of money was made.

The view from the top was one of the best I had seen in England despite the haze from hundreds of fires. There was enough flat grass for the children to run and crawl. The city lay all about cradled by distant hills. I showed Ailgifu the ditch, but, as she said, if you hadn't known what had happened there, you would never have guessed.

I knelt, said the *Lord's Prayer* and goodbye to Waltheof. He left my dreams.

The following days Odo was often in Winchester acting as joint regent while William continued to stay in Normandy. In fact, William had been so little in England after his son's death in the forest that he was virtually an absent ruler. Every few months on his tours of the country, Odo would call me to the suite he kept at the palace. Increasingly, it seemed Odo saw little difference between his rooms and the empty royal apartments. Lēofric and I formed one of a cadre of trusted messengers who carried notes to those nobles and land-holding knights who formed the inner core of Odo's political strength. I was always under strict instruction to destroy these missives if there was any chance of their loss.

It was a pleasant period. The weather was usually good, the countryside was quiet and we had a strong permanent escort. We were often away for a week at a time and saw many towns – Exeter, Bristol, Durham, Norwich, York – which had previously only been names to us. All had their attractions, although York, rapidly being rebuilt, was always our favourite. To our disappointment, we were never asked to go to London.

We also met many of our hosts and, as the bishop's representatives, sometimes joined them at table and heard their drunken conversation. It was clear that William's absences, and his high taxes, had made the king increasingly unpopular. Much of the debate was of the eventual succession. There was great sympathy for William's estranged eldest son, Robert Curthose, always in Normandy, who would likely be deprived of his rightful inheritance. Few argued for William Rufus with many disturbed by his flagrant homosexuality. Some talked of direct action. The youngest son, Henry, was never mentioned. We took care never to discuss what we heard whilst in earshot of anyone else.

On one of our return trips, suitably separated from our soldiers, we broached what was becoming uppermost in our minds.

'There's no doubt,' started Lēofric. 'No doubt at all. We are in the middle of a conspiracy. Something is going on. Odo is setting up a series of arrangements. He is up to something.'

'We need to be very careful we are not caught up in whatever it is,' I responded.

'Odo is in a dangerous mood,' continued Lēofric. 'I sometimes think he is going mad: the way he talks, flaunts himself, falls into rages, his short temper. I think he is a man who has lost his purpose. He has more land and property than he knows what to do with. What good is another jewelled cup or another lobster? He has built his magnificent new cathedral and adorned it with his wonder in its nave. He is a bishop who can rise no further because Lanfranc is in his way and there is no love lost between them. He is a great earl and how can an earl rise without being in the royal line?'

'Perhaps he wants to be king,' I quipped, 'or even pope?'

'Do you know,' said Lēofric, 'you could be right.'

We rode for a distance in silence.

'What if all our messages are about setting up a coup for when William dies? Odo could have made an arrangement with Robert Curthose. We know he disapproves of Rufus. On the other hand, we also know from what we have heard that there is serious trouble with the papacy and the right to be pope is being bought and sold. Do not forget that Norman princes have now captured most of southern and central Italy, as well as Sicily. Could Odo be planning something in Rome? He is certainly wealthy and vain enough.'

Sometimes it is unwise to speculate. The thought can become master to the deed. In the morning, two days after our latest return, replies delivered, I was wakened at my home by Hugh de Port in person.

'Listen, Gilbert, you and I are in great danger. You know I am lord of the Isle of Wight. I am ordered there with a force of men under instruction from William who is in Normandy. I am to arrest Odo who is on the island waiting for a favourable wind and I must hold him until William arrives in person. I do not know who I can trust. Odo has not shared anything with me, but I know his messengers, like you, have been travelling the whole country over the last months.

'Do you know what is going on? If this thing, whatever it is, unravels it could mean the death of all Odo's servants who are close to him and do his bidding.'

I shook my head in wonderment and denial.

'We ride for Southampton and the Wight at once,' Hugh continued. 'You are coming with me. I may need your fast and devious talking.'

When Hugh arrested Odo at supper in the port of Freshwater, I thought he would wither on the spot under the bishop's glare. I tried to stay in the background, but Odo fixed me also. I knew that if ever he had power over me in the future, I, and all my family, were dead.

Hugh sent for reinforcements and there was a great melee when William arrived direct from Normandy the next day. Odo was given short shrift and taken to Winchester. His few supporters and servants drifted quietly away. Hugh made sure that William knew that he and his men were not implicated, identifying us with a sweep of his hand. I was gratified that at the moment William seemed not to care. He had wrath only for for his half-brother.

It became clear from the trial in Council which Hugh attended that Odo had raised a private army; a large number of knights had been recruited, but for what purpose was never stated and we never found out. William charged Odo with arrogance, maladministration and taking knights away from England when they were needed for its defence. His offence had been committed as earl of Kent and not as a bishop, although I heard that this device was invented by

Lanfranc in order to separate any interference from the church in Normandy or Rome. Lanfranc wrote to Odo, 'You have acted unworthily, putting worldly considerations before the law of God and having insufficient regard for the honour due to a priest.'

What was clear was that Odo had upset the king so profoundly that William intended to imprison him for the rest of his life. Odo was taken to Rouen where his ship sailed directly through the castle river gate and he was transferred to some little comfort in the old tower.

I was still shaking when I recounted the story to Ailgifu. I hoped against hope that we had escaped William's anger as he was a vicious man when crossed. Various abbots and some men of rank were quickly removed. I was without an income although my chests and a store at Medstead were comfortably full. I didn't see Odo leave Winchester. In fact, I hid indoors at the appointed time, [*and never saw him again although Lēofric did in most strange circumstances*].

All observers agreed that Odo sought new challenges which involved even more power. There were two rumours as to what had been Odo's plan. Both were discussed endlessly by those who thought they knew what had happened. Both were also so close to our own speculations that we went cold with the memory.

In the first, Odo had ambitions to become pope by using bribery and the threat of violence to fix elections. The papal court of Gregory VII was known as venal and ripe for take over. Odo's 'goodly company of distinguished knights' was to go with him to Rome, where he had bought a palace, furnishing it at great expense and fortifying it. Odo would join with fellow resident Normans, mainly some of the dozen Hauteville brothers from the peninsula around Cherbourg, close friends of Geoffrey de Montbray, and enforce his ambition.

In the second, Odo was anticipating William's early death, although he could not have known the date in advance unless he intended regicide. Odo's personal army was to join with Robert Curthose and be ready to seize the moment. Presumably, though, Robert would have something to say about losing his own right to the royal succession in favour of his uncle?

Lēofric and I agreed easily. It was time to lay low. Luck doesn't last for ever. We spent the next few weeks in Medstead.

9 DOMESDAY AND DECEPTION, 1083-1086

Villagers all around Medstead had only a vague idea that something serious had happened at the heart of the Norman invaders. Ailgifu told the story of Odo's disappearance into a prison in Rouen to her family and friends. She was met with shrugs and careless stares. Odo, in power or not, was neither here nor there in the daily lives of people who tilled fields and herded cattle. What mattered was filling their hungry bellies and grappling with water shortages.

Belief in the king's total control was fundamental to Norman confidence. The open threat from one of their own was a blow to the *solar plexus*. Lēofric and I agreed that despite William's decisive response the reign had lost its certainty. When William died, change would be far-reaching and unlikely to be for the better. Odo had placed an early marker for his support for Robert Curthose, William's eldest son, in any battle for the succession. We knew from our own travels that many leading Normans agreed with him and, under the right circumstances, would be prepared to fight. Paradoxically, the next surviving son, William Rufus, had support among the native English. Henry Beauclerc, the youngest boy, who like both of his brothers had been tutored by Lanfranc, did not enter the conversations.

The death of queen Matilda next year, 1083, left William distraught. He vowed to give up hunting in her memory, his most precious activity. The death also marked a further deterioration in relations between the king and his eldest son. Matilda was well known as a buffer between the two. Robert relied on her support when dealing with his father's constant scorn. With Odo in prison, Robert was now alone among those close to William. The stubborn young man contemptuously refused to follow or obey his father; the quick-tempered king continually poured abuse and reproach on him in public.

While all this swirled in the background, it continued obvious to me that the Norman elite was corrupt almost without exception. They respected power for its own sake and that made them careful to keep malfeasance undetected. However, fear of punishment did not soften the essential bankruptcy of their moral code. William was a crook interested in the acquisition of ever more wealth. His landowning barons would conceal as much as possible from the king while using his techniques to steal from their own tenants, those very people they had sworn to protect with their knightly vows. And so it went down the social scale until one reached the nadir of the invaders' influence. Most bishops, irreligious and indecent, were worse for they took lands, property and taxes, even from those who had little or nothing, while they hid behind holy robes and righteousness.

I am not saying, because I do not know, that the Normans were the worst in the world at their primary trade. However, I was assured by daily comments that, as a matter of course, the Normans reached further with regular, rapacious deeds than the Anglo-Saxon aristocrats. What I do suggest is that every time you grasped hands with a Norman, you should count your fingers afterwards.

Lēofric, of course, had come to the same conclusion even before Hastings. He would often point to the half-Norman pseudo saint, king Edward, as totally corrupted by the flood of foreigners he welcomed into his court. If further proof were needed, he added, one had only to look at the congregation and clergy of the Old Minster.

My young friend's answer was to learn the skill of swordplay. He found the poorest Norman knight in Winchester, freshly arrived, and persuaded him to give lessons. At Lēofric's earnest request, I attended the practices twice in a quiet field a mile outside the city walls. I admit, but not to his face, that Lēofric was a natural. On my second outing, I was persuaded to try my luck. I was humiliated by his speed, power and anticipation. Ailgifu and Mildgyth thought the whole idea likely to upset any drunken, passing Norman lout. I agreed. It was all I could do to persuade Lēofric not to wear his new toy within the city. Ailgifu took it as the worst sign when he sat in the garden into the evening sharpening and polishing the already gleaming surface of his weapon.

For my part, I decided to look for some work from a new sponsor. My money was not within sight of running out, but there could come a day. There were many among William's secular servants who carried out the mundane tasks of organising the conquest who owed their positions to Odo. It was true that most of us kept a little quiet about our first sponsor after the bishop's ignominious departure. There was a rumour of a new man who was making an impression in William's chancery who had a special skill with tax collection. His name was

Ranulf. His nickname *Flambard*, devouring flame, came from his quick-burning temper. By early reputation, he was, like me, an archetypal, low-born professional administrator who, unlike me I hoped, upset the Norman elite with his lack of respect. Just twenty-five, he was a hard man and business-like in dealing with civil and ecclesiastical questions.

I wondered if Ranulf might need some help. I also thought I might know him.

He sat, quill in hand, frowning over some leases. His black hair was cropped in the Norman fashion which unfortunately, to my view, accented his large eyes. He would certainly be good looking to the ladies. He was fit, lean, in fact, every inch the soldier rather than a clerk. He acknowledged me with an impatient grunt made without looking up. I introduced myself and asked if his father was the parish priest named Thurstin from near Bayeux.

That caught his attention. He looked at me and nodded.

'Your father taught me when I was a boy,' I explained. 'I often held you in my arms and rocked you to sleep. My name is Gilbert. How is your father?'

'You'll have to be faster than that these days to get the better of me,' he responded, but it was said with a smile. He offered his hand without rising. 'Thank you for looking after me. Sadly, my father is dead of disease. He died a poor but holy man, well-loved I was told. I have heard mention of you, Gilbert, as a man of intelligence who speaks many languages and who can be trusted. What can I do for you?'

'I am looking for work,' I explained. 'I hoped that you might have some suggestions. I need to help my wife, Ailgifu. She has lost half of her bees to this winter's frosts. Bees are now expensive and in short supply.'

He grinned again. 'This Ailgifu would be the maker of our noble king's favourite honey? Did you know some of her pots have followed him to Rouen?'

Ranulf became instantly focussed and serious. He gave me a short lecture while staring out of the casement.

'Our beloved Lord, the king, has described two major problems that today threaten his realm.

'The first is straightforward and may well be known to you. It is not my personal concern. England has endured two conquests, Danish and Norman, in less than fifty years. The native population's resistance did not succeed in either case. Another invasion is threatened by the Danes, this time allied with count Robert of Flanders. Cnut, grandnephew of Cnut the Great, who recently ruled

England, considers the crown of England to be rightfully his and regards our gracious king as a usurper. He is readying a fleet of, perhaps, a thousand ships to take the whole country. William needs cash for military works and ships. He sees this as a chance to end this northern nonsense once and for all.'

Ranulf turned around quickly to see if I was paying sufficient attention. I passed the test.

'The second problem is more subtle,' he continued, 'but ends in the same requirement for taxation. The king needs to set a final seal on what, we must be honest, is still an unpopular conquest. Challenges to William's legal status are still whispered, even close to home. It is vital that his churchmen, our damned lawyers, see him as the undisputed legal successor. William met with his major clergy, landholders and sheriffs, at an impressive feast at Gloucester this Christmas past. It was agreed that there will be a great survey of the whole country that will decide where wealth and land is allocated. It will resolve disputes among our thieving barons. It will bring the subjected people under the rule of new written law. The survey book will be the basis for all future taxation. Its pages will be the final touch that will reset the clock on the king's control of all English land.

'It will also be,' and here the smile came back, 'a great opportunity for those who administer it.' A pause. 'Would you like to assist me?'

I didn't see there was much of a choice. I could decline and make another life-long enemy. I could accept and try to affect the result to the benefit of all those who mattered to me. It would also mean good employment. I told Ranulf that I would be happy to join him. I laid out that part of my experience which I thought would benefit the project. I told him that I had working for me an English clerk, well-versed in Winchester's archives, whose language skills and contacts would be of great use.

'Come back tomorrow and give me your first thoughts,' he ordered.

I bowed to yet another man who had risen above me. Without really directing my path, I found my way to the clearing outside the walls and waited until Lēofric had finished banging his sword against the increasingly useless defence of the young Norman knight.

'You need a new playmate,' I told him. 'If you carry on with this novice, you'll get arrogant and begin to think that you are better than you really are.'

He gave me a light touch with the flat of his sword on my bottom.

'You're probably right. You've got a gleam in your eye, Gilbert. What have you really come to tell me?'

A half an hour later, Lēofric gave a great sigh.

'Couldn't you have found a larger project?' he moaned. 'We'll be at this for years. But, of course, having asked, you had no option but to accept. And, we should be able to do some good behind everyone's back. We need pen and mead and to set down some thoughts for Master Ranulf.'

The following day, we presented Ranulf with a parchment with our efforts. He read it very slowly then picked up his own quill and read it again, making marks, the odd tick and cross, the addition of a few words.

'Excellent work, Gilbert,' he grunted. 'Congratulations to you and your English assistant here, Lēofric, isn't it. I shall have to keep a close eye on you both.'

We look pleased and yet respectful.

'Before any details, I want to make one thing clear. This is to be my project. I will lead. I will get the credit and it will make my career. If I am successful, you will be well remunerated. I can be even clearer. All the information from the survey will pass through this office. I will see it all. You will not notice when I make the odd alteration. This is my opportunity and I intend to take it. I look for loyalty. Is that acceptable to you both?'

We both nodded while trying to look like honest and loyal men who could be trusted to corrupt the books. I had already underestimated Ranulf. He was clearly ruthless and determined, a typical newly-arrived crooked Norman determined to make his fortune. If we stood in his way, or crossed him, we would be crushed. But, he was also a most capable administrator and we would need to run to keep up with him.

The country was split into seven circuits, each of which had its own group of supervising commissioners or specially appointed clerks of the court. Some of these would be typically venal, others would want to show a determined search for the truth. To speed up this process, Ranulf planned to use the shire courts and, where necessary, place them under duress. He had acquired a large number of king's messengers to deliver standardised forms which would be filled in and sworn to by the local lords and authorities before jurors. The results could be subject to review if there was any hint of false information.

Impressively, Ranulf had agreed with Samson of Bayeux, another of Odo's prodigies, to be the scribe for the whole enterprise. Samson, a royal chaplain, had trained at Liège with his brother, Thomas, now archbishop of York.

'There is a bishopric for Samson when he completes his scribbling,' added Ranulf. 'I hear he has his eye on Worcester. He is ready to begin. The work will be that of a single man and written in Latin.

'Our job in Winchester is to mobilise the predominantly English and Anglo-Danish population so that they co-operate in the king's remarkable survey with all its communication difficulties and lack of native incentive. I want a minutely ordered bureaucratic enterprise. Bluntly, we will give the king an authoritative legal framework that will subjugate a peace-hungry, productive and taxable society.

'No one except the king will possess a title to property earlier than 1066. Everyone's rights will stem from the conquest. There will be no other authority and no prior claims.'

Ranulf gave us our tasks based on our recommendations. We had scored a major advantage with the timing of my approach for work.

The survey would not spring out of thin air. The skeletal records of liabilities of counties and estates, held in the minsters, would provide a framework. We were to explore these records and make them useful.

We were to agree the format of the questionnaire with Ranulf using as a base the decisions made in Gloucester.

Next, from our table in Winchester, we were to control the process of data collection. This meant listing and despatching the questionnaires, recording their return, showing them to Ranulf for his approval, sending them on to Samson for scribing, checking his work and collecting his pages into, it was planned, a single book.

'There is an additional task, here,' observed Ranulf. 'For two decades, obedient executors of the king's will, with the ruler often absent, and working for rapacious lords and bishops like Odo, have transferred the possession of thousands of acres. Many of these officials have already been publicly exposed in open court, accused of putting three acres here or fifteen acres there in the wrong hands or grabbing it for themselves. While they cannot all be brought to justice, they can be made to feel the heat of knowledge.

'I expect a stream of special pleadings made by the bullies and the guilty. You will conduct these first interviews and, initially, reject them. Should the pressure become too great or serious bribes be offered, you will pass individual cases to me.'

Ranulf offered a final homily. 'In the Last Judgement, Christ in majesty will judge the living and the dead. So will the king's great survey. We will compare information about who held the land at the invasion with the dead of battle, with those landowners who were killed or died between then and now, as well as the living who lay claim today. The text will serve as a final judgement about every disputed property.'

He weighed the effect of his words on us and then stood up with arms wide.

'How about a drink, boys?' he asked. 'I've got some local girls in my chambers with some food and musicians. A good carousal is meat for the soul, yes?'

Here was the other side of Ranulf's character that I realised we would have to get used to during the project. We managed to escape this time as the man was soon lost in a whirl of self-indulgence. It was a contrast that I could never get used to: Ranulf had great skill and high ambition, wrapped in piety, but yet he was regularly subsumed in an addiction to lust, over eating and acts of individual cruelty. Many young females left his rooms in need of tending.

Despite Ranulf's close attention, we were able to make some useful adjustments to the survey. Overall, he organised seventeen, well-spread, small estates in the south of the country for himself with only three of them in Hampshire, just small farms at Great Funtley near Wickham, and Beckley and Bile in the New Forest. His main concern was Corston in Wiltshire and his manors at Guildford, Godalming and nearby Tuesley, all held directly from the king. He was particularly nervous of these last in Surrey and any others locally where bishop Walkelin showed any interest. There was little love lost between them. We were deputed to keep a close watch on developments and, as a result, managed to maintain administrative management of the lands from Alresford north to Medstead, including Ropley, and into Surrey. I had Ailgifu's bees at heart and freeholdings to protect.

Walkelin claimed the whole of Alresford as the lord of right stating categorically that the land had always belonged to the church of Winchester from time immemorial and most recently by Stigand. He offered no proof. In fact, he got angry when it was requested.

Walkelin's next move was to try to stall the inclusion of Winchester in the survey. His public argument was that as London was not part of the exercise, neither should Winchester as it was the capital city. As William had called for completion within a year, the bishop's prevarication was successful. He bought time to conduct his own audit of the episcopal estates so that misappropriations could be disguised. It was clear to us that Walkelin had a cathedral to complete and the money was not going to come from his own pocket. What did surprise us was that Ranulf accepted this obvious subterfuge without debate. He was instructed to be thorough and that included sending a second set of commissioners to check suspect responses and to report culprits directly to the king. There was some *quid pro quo* with Walkelin somewhere, but we couldn't find it. Nor did we want to stir resentment by pressing the case.

Walkelin's returns for his estates outside Winchester were collected in our office where we set about making corrections. We were also instructed by Ranulf to abridge records by omitting both livestock and the population at invasion. We were never told the reason, but Lēofric was convinced it was to cover up the devastation wrought by William in the harrowing of the north.

The enormity of Walkelin's estates was breathtaking. He held some two hundred manors, overwhelmingly in Hampshire and close by, but with large scatterings across most counties. Their combined value at the time of the survey in 1085 was around £1,250. The church in Hampshire was twice as wealthy as the king and there were few single manors in the county.

We decided our best riposte was to lessen the value of Alresford, which included Medstead, and its three churches, and thereby reduce potential taxation on the villagers. Walkelin was unlikely to know where Medstead was even when he passed close by on his journeys to London. Fifty hides became forty-two. The land worked forty ploughs instead of fifty, the sixty villagers dropped to forty-eight, and the forty-four smallholders to thirty-six. We also misplaced some slaves, two mills, meadow acreage and a lot of pigs in pasture. While the whole manor had been worth £6 a year, we placed the rent at £4 because the area 'could not bear it for long'. This fall in rent value was quite common. Any casual observer of the returns could easily use these numbers to work out the path of the invading armies twenty years before. The devastation they caused to villages as they passed was still not repaired. In contrast, Bishop's Sutton admitted a large appreciation from £50 to £60.

When our misreporting was all done, we destroyed Walkelin's parchment return and forged a new one of our own so that no blame could fall on us. It couldn't have been simpler as we made our changes after the commissioners' scrutiny was finished.

Next came Odo who was still reputed to be the second largest landowner across the country after the king. Perhaps there wasn't time to show confiscations, but his return still listed over seven hundred properties, the greater number flowing from his earldom of Kent.

Hugh de Port was lord of lands in Kent, Surrey and a comparatively meagre forty-six manors in Hampshire, all these last from Odo. We noted that many of his Hampshire properties were near to Medstead and Ropley, like Alton, Binsted, Bramley, Chawton, Dummer, Neatham and Preston Candover. After a long discussion one evening, we decided to leave these as they were. Who knew when we might need Hugh's help?

Hugh was also one of fifteen sheriffs named more than once for their misdeeds in land appropriation. The great majority of these concerned only small pieces, ancillary portions of manors or plots of small freeholders. Hugh's stolen lands were so small that they hardly seemed worthy of official pursuit. We were left in no doubt that the finished book, monumental though it may be, could never be regarded as a wholly truthful document. It enclosed too many vested interests.

All of which left us with Sutton which contained Ropley in addition to Bighton, Bramdean, West Tisted and, separated, Headley. Here, we had several strokes of luck which made us think God was on our side. The land had been held before the conquest by the English king, Harold, and he was no longer around to contradict anything we might introduce.

Next, Samson had made one of his few scribing errors for the county and it was a big one. His numbering had slipped over four consecutive estates, one of which was for the manor of *Sudtone* in the hundred of *Esselai*, the old names for Sutton and Ashley. In addition, the landholder, count Eustace, was omitted and the allocation made wrongly to earl Roger de Montgomery of Shrewsbury.

This error worked for us in two ways. First, earl Roger had no claim to the land and would not be looking for a record or a financial return. Second, Léofric and I both knew a deal about count Eustace of Boulogne and we bet that he would not be watching his English interests with care.

Eustace, once brother-in-law to Edward the Confessor, was notorious as a coward among the tight-knit invasion crowd, the knights who had accompanied William to Hastings. On one of the panels on the Bayeux embroidery, Eustace was shown pointing frantically to the rear and encouraging William to retreat from the battle as it was lost. Eustace was named above in Latin, but he was also easily identified. His nickname was Eustace *aux Grenons*, long moustaches. Eustace was immediately wounded in the back and covered in blood so that the men near William thought the king killed. In an adjacent embroidery, the duke is shown raising his helmet to reassure his soldiers and then to lead them to victory.

Despite this loss of face, Eustace was gifted substantial lands to recognise his contribution of fifty boats and fifty knights to the armada. Eustace thought the lands inadequate and, in pique the next year, he joined with men of Kent to try to seize Dover Castle. I suspect that he saw the potential joining of Dover with Boulogne as giving him serious prestige. The fight for Dover failed, put down by Adam fitz Hubert, and Eustace's English lands were confiscated. After reconciliation with William, only Sutton and Neatham were returned. Eustace's time was then concentrated in Boulogne where his French domains were under attack from all sides.

As a result of Eustace's absence, his small English estates were lying largely unattended and had slipped into disarray. Without a formal entry in the *Winchester Book*, as we had come to call the survey, rents might lay unclaimed for years to come. By some slight amendments, we could make the position worse. It was certainly worth a try.

That year was a crisis year as William scrabbled for money to pay for mercenaries to counter the Danes. William normally collected Danegeld at a rate of two shillings on the hide, but with an invasion pending, and perhaps further retaliations around Normandy in 1086, it was taken at six shillings. Wealth in England was concentrated in so few hands. We estimated that in the year of the Book, there were some 2,000 foreign knights among about 10,000 settlers controlling a population of one and a half million. William and his family possessed about one fifth of the land, the church about a quarter and ten senior barons another quarter. When you got down to it, the country was controlled by about 250 individuals. It was no surprise that the farming community was taxed to the hilt, their rents raised to the maximum tolerable and even above.

Mercenaries had to be housed somewhere and, while the major forces were placed in the midlands and the north to be ready for the Danes, small groups were allocated around Winchester which would be less at threat in the immediate aftermath of a landing. The Norman soldiery at Medstead fort were withdrawn and a detachment of twenty Franconians billeted there.[1] The local community was charged with their upkeep which caused great stress on scarce provisions. Everyone took to enjoying the king's venison from Chawton woods. A similar number of men from Gascony were housed near the old Roman encampment not far from where Ailgifu kept her hives at Ropley.

At first the incomers caused continuing tension, especially as they looked to villagers for food to serve their conspicuous appetites. Lēofric solved the problem by a weekly cart of provisions only delivered if the peace was kept and the hives guarded. Both parties were gone within six months without any harm done unless one counted the four babies that appeared eight months later who, fatherless, brought fresh blood into the two communities.

Ranulf passed on with some fervour the deadlines he had been set by William for the completion of the *Winchester Book*. It never looked like we would meet the target until at Christmas, with three months to spare, the project was split into two. The *Little Book* held all the information for the economically advanced and socially complex areas of East Anglia and Essex which were giving us so many administrative problems. The high number of small landholders complicated the tenanted records.

This was a smart move by Ranulf. First and foremost, of course, it allowed him to sidestep any potential failure, and, second, it immediately cut out a lot of the travelling. The transfer was made easier because my old friend Adam was one of the commissioners.

Our copy of the *Great Book* was kept in the king's treasury at Winchester. A steady flow of sheep skins, amounting eventually to almost two hundred, arrived every day from the pen of Samson. It was truly a book of wonder and, towards the end, we allocated time each noon for all those who wished to queue to be astonished.

William planned a great climax when the *Winchester Book* was finished, held at his new castle at Sarum at the beginning of August in 1086. Ranulf made a meal

---

1 Franconian: A person from Franken, an historic region of Germany now part of Bavaria, Thuringia and Baden-Württemberg.

of inviting me and, by inference, not Lēofric. Even Ailgifu begrudgingly saw this as a great honour. Lēofric was far less respectful.

All the king's counsellors, all the people of any account who held land from all over England, were summoned. The party from Winchester was over a thousand strong with armed escorts, retainers and hangers-on. We followed the Roman road from the city to Sarum. I saw the king only from a distance. It was remarkable how obese this once great fighting man had become. However, I did have a kind of pride of place. I rode beside Ranulf and had command of six men who surrounded a festooned and polished cart that carried the *Great Book*. The book was held in an ornate chest that suggested to me the great Ark of the Jewish Covenant.

It was a blisteringly hot day in a very thundery year with much flooding and many people killed by lightning. There was a great famine bringing pestilence and, for me at least, it was sickening to see evidence of this as we made our royal progress.

The heat allowed the ceremony to be held in the bailey; not even the new great hall could have coped. All men there submitted to William with oaths of allegiance that lorded over those made previously to all other men. The acclamation was made in three great roars. Although, perforce, I had to join in, I was less committed and able to look around. Several men of rank gave their roar and then spat onto the ground. Others held their hands with fingers crossed behind their backs in remembrance of the old Christian symbol which recognised God above all others.

As if it was all planned, and I am sure it was, just as the last roar died away, a royal messenger arrived on a remarkably fresh horse. He brought news in a document taken straight to the king. It was read discretely to William for his skill with letters was limited. He began to laugh, long and hard, and I imagined his fat rolling under his silks. All in the bailey were confused and unsure whether to join in the jollity or to wait for more information.

Slowly, word spread and the din became immense as the full import became clear. Cnut, the great king of the Danes, had been assassinated by rebels in his own country a few weeks before. He was slaughtered with his brother Benjamin and seventeen followers in front of the altar of St Alban's Priory in Odense. The army and fleet intended to invade England had disbanded.

I wondered whether the *Great Book* had been constructed in vain and the sweeping Sarum oath taken unnecessarily. But, of course, I realised immediately that once an instrument of taxation had been created, a use would always be found for it by those in government.

On the way home, an excited Ranulf assured me that I had been accorded a noteworthy privilege by attending, perhaps, the greatest ceremony in Norman and English history. Under his patronage, I would now be seen as one of the core administrators of the Norman empire. We were riding past some starving crofters. I wasn't that impressed, but nodded to show my gratitude. Ranulf prayed for William's long life and his own continuing advancement.

I heard within the week that William had left Winchester for Normandy with as much treasure as he could carry. Ailgifu counted our large purse of silver. Lēofric supped his mead and hoped that we had all seen the last of our royal lord.

10 THE THEFT OF ALRESFORD, 1087-1093

The brothers Adam and Eudo Dapifer were unexpectedly and excitedly in Winchester in September 1087. They and others brought a stream of information which shocked and unnerved the city. With knights, clerks and messengers, I took to haunting the palace grounds while we waited for more news. Ailgifu demanded that Lēofric escort her, the children and Mildgyth to the recently completed house at Ropley for safety 'while these Normans played their games'.

William, our king, was dead. His second surviving son, William Rufus, had claimed the throne and was making rapid arrangements to cement his authority. He was expected in Winchester within the hour, perhaps that day, certainly within the week.

The revelations came to us in bits and pieces that were not in the order of their happening. I witnessed none of the main events except when the new king finally arrived amidst a clatter of hooves on a tired horse, sheathed in white sweat. I want to write down briefly what I heard, but did not see.

William had declared war in the Vexin, a county on the River Seine, which the French king Philip had seized and was using to make raids into Normandy. William acted with typical brutality when he fired the town of Mantes; two renowned religious hermits were killed deliberately.

The pommel of William's saddle ripped into his stomach as he tried to leap a ditch. He was moved from Rouen to the quiet of the priory of St-Gervais. Many clergy and family, principally his sons William and Henry, gathered as he lay dying in great pain. He was said to have panicked then calmed himself as death approached. He made gifts to religious institutions for the good of his soul and ordered that in England each church should receive sixty pence and the poor in each county should be given one hundred pounds.

A royal death was usually accompanied by the release of all political prisoners. William agreed but with one exception: bishop Odo, his half-brother, was to stay in the castle prison at Rouen. William prophesised calamity if Odo were set free.

141

I am amazed that you do not appreciate what kind of man is this for whom you plead. Are you not interceding for a man who has long been an enemy of the church and a cunning instigator of treacherous rebellion? Have I not kept under restraint for four years this bishop who, when he should have been a most just viceroy in England, became the worst oppressor of the people and destroyer of monasteries? I have imprisoned not a bishop but a tyrant. If he goes free, without doubt, he will disturb the whole kingdom and bring thousands to destruction.

This act of prescience or revenge by William was eventually rescinded after pressure from Odo's other brother, Count Robert of Mortain.

Unwillingly I grant that my brother may be released from prison, but I warn you that he will be the cause of death and grievous harm to many.

At this dire warning, I shared a glance with Lēofric as we both wondered if we might be on Odo's list for retribution when he was freed. I was now into my forties and not inclined to prolonged hiding. Suddenly, Ropley didn't seem far enough away. I was scared for Ailgifu and our children.

Normandy was bequeathed to Robert, but there was doubt to the last whether he would be disinherited. William Rufus was nominated for England and given a sealed letter to archbishop Lanfranc ordering that arrangements for a rapid coronation should be made. Henry was given money.

William died soon after dawn on the Thursday. There was panic. All expected troubled times and prepared as they thought best. Attendants wandered dazed having lost their lifetime leader. Others rode to protect their own property. Yet others looted the death chamber. The burial by all accounts was bizarre. The body lay abandoned for many hours. Later in the day, it was cleansed by the Rouen clergy and then sailed to Caen down the River Orne for a ceremony at the abbey church of St-Etienne. One of the town houses caught fire during the procession burning down neighbouring properties. Odo was among those present, already released. As the corpse was placed in full view on its coffin in the abbey, one of the congregation rose to claim that the land on which they all stood had been stolen from his father by William before 1066. The man spoke the truth and was given money in hurried embarrassment. As William was lowered into the tomb which was too small, his body burst open. A stench filled the church. The priests concluded the rites quickly and fled.

'He was not a great king,' declared Lēofric, 'but we may end up with worse. I think he was morally and intellectually inferior to all his Norse ancestors who governed England. He was astute, but not wise; strong, certainly, but without any real purpose. *Limited* is the best word. Everyone I knew who met him said he was narrow, ignorant and superstitious.'

We never could work out what route the eighteen-year-old William Rufus took to England. Rufus didn't wait for his father's death. The unkind said that he made haste to the sand dune port of Wissant till word reached him. Eudo, ever loyal to those in power, would say no more than he was present at the death and then rode quickly to ensure that the royal castles at Dover, Pevensey and Hastings were secure for the new monarch. Among the fast-riding king's party was Robert Bloet, a trusted chaplain of the Conqueror, known to Lanfranc as the king's man of confidence, and who carried the sealed letter and authority. After some protracted bargaining on church rights and William's commitment to good behaviour, Lanfranc agreed to perform the coronation. Bloet was rewarded with the bishopric of Lincoln.

I do know that Adam rode to be with the king at Winchester where they were met by a confident Walkelin, Hugh de Port and a salivating Ranulf, each offering their obedience and service. Two hostages, brought over from France after being freed at William's deathbed, were reincarcerated in the city in a ruthless demonstration of power. The first was Wulnoth Godwinson who had been an almost perpetual prisoner since he was taken aged eleven in 1051 in the everlasting game of thrones. No vestige of the claims of Edith or her brother, the dead king Harold, could be left to chance. The other was earl Morcar of York, an aging aspirant and discontent who had refused to join Harold at Hastings and thereby condemned him to defeat. After several rebellions and reconciliations, including the failed defence of Ely with Hereward the Wake, William had Morcar taken to Normandy.

Another earl, Roger of Hereford, imprisoned from the plot that saw Waltheof lose his head in front of me on St Giles Hill, was dragged from prison to suffer the same fate. The return of cast off memories brought several sleepless nights.

Despite the mayhem, William's main reason to visit Winchester was to seize his father's fortune. Ranulf told me it was impossible for any man to say how much was gathered. The king spent several hours in the treasure room picking up one precious thing wrapped in purple cloth after another and running his hands through gold and silver coin and jewels alike. William claimed it all, after honouring his father's bequests, and the remainder provided the foundation of his power throughout his reign.

The coronation took place in Westminster abbey on a Sunday, less than three weeks after William began his madcap rides, channel crossing and city visits. Lanfranc performed the ceremony under Anglo-Saxon liturgy. William walked past the tomb of his distant kinsman, Edward the Confessor, and stood where the usurper Harold was also crowned. There was no time to arrange new regalia and so what had sufficed for others had to make do.

Like his father, William Rufus was mentally and physically strong, a fine soldier. He was also illiterate like all his brothers. Whereas his father was dour, this son was more humorous with a particular liking for shocking high-principled clerics like Walkelin. High on Walkelin's list of improprieties was William's notorious homosexuality. His red complexion and tinged hair jarred and was seen to add to the insult. The aging Walkelin learned early in the reign to control his sniffy displeasure when William was in the room. He recognised the new king's heartless streak and knew, if he was to keep his position, he needed to be appreciated for his spotless honesty. For a man of years with the bishop's record, all agreed that this would be difficult. The king's dissolute and rapacious court was much more to Ranulf's liking.

Within a week, I was called from Ropley to Walkelin's private sanctum. I had never been to the bishop's palace nor had I met the man and yet he knew of me and where to find me. The meeting lasted less than five minutes and changed my life.[1]

I was taken to meet Godfrey, the prior, from Cambrai and another man I had not met and who was, as with much of the housing around, landlord of my Winchester home. There was the briefest of pleasantries.

'My Lord Walkelin needs you to perform a task, Gilbert,' he began. 'It will not be difficult for you and your Saxon servant, but it requires complete discretion from you both. Your work on the *Great Book* makes you ideally qualified as does your knowledge of the villages of Medstead and Ropley. You will remember that

---

1   Editor's note: Gilbert's description of the meeting has been placed in the preface for literary effect.

the church in Winchester claims all the land of the manor of Alresford, held by the bishop from time immemorial?'

I remembered the angry response from the palace when Lēofric and I had challenged the claim. Like all these duplicitous clergymen, Godfrey never actually said what he meant. The prior's language was tortuous. Perhaps, it was his life-long training? Perhaps, it was so he could deny that he had said what he wanted me to know? I deciphered the message. Walkelin had lied when he told the old king of the bishopric's ownership. There were no charters, no records. At some point since the invasion, the land had been stolen. The new king was in a determined mood and ready to show his royal strength. Walkelin, amongst many others, had been asked to prove their grand assertions of ownership. The bishop was not yet charged, but he was worried, possibly frightened and certainly guilty. I suspected Ranulf's vengeful hand behind the scenes.

Godfrey, the prior, finally got to the nub.

'The church's records are incomplete, Gilbert. You are to find the charter or charters that are missing and place them in the files of the *Winchester Book* so that they can easily be uncovered. This work will come from Saxon times and should be impeccable. Do you understand?'

I nodded. The church was asking me to become a forger for its Norman bishop's financial benefit and to save him from disgrace.

'I do not need to see what you find,' concluded Godfrey. 'Just let me know by short letter when the task is complete. You have four weeks. You will be well remunerated. Do not discuss this, ah, search with anyone except your servant, not your wife nor anyone else who occupies my house in Scowrtenestret where you live. You will be responsible for this silence.

'Thank you for visiting with us today.'

He gave me his blessing and left me alone. I rode slowly back to Ropley for a serious family meeting.

'I suppose we have to see this as an opportunity,' began Lēofric.

'Opportunity!' exploded Ailgifu. 'These monsters in skirts are threatening to throw us out of our house in Winchester if you do not do what they ask. Then, they will stop all work for you two conspirators. Then, as they have stolen Medstead, they'll close down my mead house and tax all my family into serfdom. Then, they might come after this house. Then, they might throw you two idiots into prison or worse. Opportunity!'

'Could be worse,' added Lēofric. 'Nobody mentioned the hives. At least the bees might survive.'

Ailgifu lost her temper and threw a cushion which knocked over some mead onto a second cushion. That startled my fourth child, called Lēofric in a moment of weakness, into a great wail which brought out a well-filled breast.

'How do we work the opportunity?' I asked. 'In our favour, the prior doesn't want to be seen anywhere near our charters, but if Ranulf, I suppose it is Ranulf, sees they do not support the church's claims all hell will break lose when Walkelin is challenged. Where's our advantage? We've got four weeks to find it.'

We sat and looked at each other. Lēofric replenished his mead. Baby Leo fell asleep, sated. Ailgifu soon followed. Mildgyth sat quiet with her darning.

I broke the silence. 'We have to give Walkelin what he has asked for,' I decided. 'At least, a charter which will pass Ranulf's scrutiny, but also one which will have within its own seeds of destruction. Lēofric you must ride the Alresford bounds with Ailgifu as your guide. Our charter must have accurate stiles and boundaries.

'To be believable, the charter must carry references to Saxon leaseholders from before the conquest. My idea is that you use Ailgifu's grandfather, Ælfric, who was an ealdorman with royal connections. Concoct a story. Prepare parchment and ink. Then wait for my return.'

'Return from where?'

'Canterbury. We need to know more about charters. We know from our work on the *Winchester Book* that forgeries abound. However, to ask for more background in the minsters would soon reach prior Godfrey. There's one man who will know the general background we need and that's abbot Scolland at Saint Augustine's Abbey. That is, if he is still alive.'

It was another harsh winter come very early. I entered the spirit-laden yew wood and, after a gap of almost twenty years, it seemed just as threatening. This time I was alone. There was no snow. The ground was needle-black and lifeless. The abbey was an altogether livelier place, well-funded, with its buildings enlarged and in fine order. It may all be in the mind, but the presence of Odo still hung in the corridors and meeting rooms as if waiting for his return. The brothers were at first nervous of letting me see Scolland. After some Norman imperiousness and laboured argument, I gained access and understood the reticence. The abbot was an old man, wizened, drained of energy and had not long to live. He recognised me, held out his arms and showed his mind was still sharp. He gleefully pointed to one of our designs for the embroidery which showed him as a witness in the upper frieze. He still loved to gossip.

I explained I needed advice of a personal nature. He tapped his nose to signify confidences and I told him enough of my story to gain his understanding.

'The church has always forged charters,' he confided. 'It is endemic. Since the Normans arrived, the forgery of charters has been the rule rather than the exception. The forgeries extend to almost all chronicles and histories. What a writer did not know, he made up, based on his faith, education and politics.

'There are many reasons, but they were mostly for the good. Some are just clumsy copies. Documents become lost and needed to be replaced. Even now, if nothing was written down, the only evidence of grants of land is in the memory of witnesses who watched a clod of earth being handed over. Gaps in imperfect title deeds for church lands need filling, especially where aged institutions are under threat. The greatest forgeries in England concerned the debate for supremacy over all the English bishops. Many papal letters to and from Canterbury, Winchester, Durham and York have been invented, more in hope than belief that they would be accepted.'

The ease with which Scolland reeled off complicit religious houses well known to him, including his own, was illuminating: Christ Church, Canterbury; Battle Abbey; Gloucester; and Ramsey Abbey. 'Of course,' he confided, 'Winchester and its minsters is a centre of proved fabrication. No document from there should be accepted at face value without close examination.'

We debated backwards and forwards and then he suddenly tired. I knew it was the last time that I would see him. His face paled.

'I cannot tell you *yes* or *no*,' he summarised. 'If your soul is with God and your charter does not endorse theft, then you have my blessing. I will tell you the trick. Make your creation boring, administrative, as if it is a simple recording. If you manage that, it is likely to be believed. However, most forgeries contain mistakes, either in the language which will be out of its age or in its lists of witnesses who may be inappropriate. The last touch is to attach a royal seal of the right period.'

He raised his hand and blessed me, then fell asleep. He was a good man.

On the ride home, I formulated my plan. It was pragmatic. We would need patience and, for it finally to have a chance of success, would need us to wait until Walkelin died.

I sent prior Godfrey in good time the shortest note that the document was lodged. A small penny purse had been sufficient to acquire the skills of a well-trained and impecunious monk knowledgeable in calligraphy. Our charter was dated 701, from the reign of Ine, king of Wessex. It granted an estate of forty hides, nearly 5,000 acres, at Alresford to the Church of Saints Peter and Paul, soon to be the growing cathedral. It confirmed a seventh century grant by Cenwalh, the king who brought Christianity to Winchester and built the Old Minster. Within the charter were the accurate boundaries of Alresford with named Saxon stiles and gates.

As Scolland predicted, our text was a little out of its time; its style was slightly flamboyant and of the tenth century. Anyone who cared to check would find the wording resembled clauses in charters from the reign of Eadgar, just over a hundred years before. The witness list was dubious and would suit a document written thirty to forty years later. The grant was supposedly confirmed by Egbert in 826, Edward the Elder in 956 and by Eadgar. All these errors were designed to be unnoticed by someone casually assessing the document in 1087, but would be uncovered by a skilled man of letters charged to investigate at a later date.

Walkelin had his proof of ownership and duly delivered a fat purse.

What no one knew except our tight group was that there was a second forged charter, but this one designed to be as believable as we could make it and certainly more authentic than the one handed to the prior. Its royal seal was a work of art and involved several nights of experiment by Mildgyth. Our second charter showed that in the late ninth or early tenth century bishop Denewulf leased the Alresford estate to a layman named Ælfred for his lifetime. In 956, king Eadwig granted the land to Ælfric, who was Ælfred's son, in a 'permanent alienation'. The land was allodial, free from any rights of a feudal landlord. Ælfric 'of Hampshire' was from royal company. From the beginning of the reign of Æthelred, the boy-king was advised by a small cabal of close kinsmen. These ealdormen were related though blood or marriage one to another. Three died or retired and Ælfric was one of the replacements in the years 982/3. His inconstancy was remarkable: fighting with the Northmen, advising the king to sue for peace. It was Ælfric who evaded leading a Hampshire army against the Danes after they had been rebuffed at Alton. He pretended to be sick and left Wilton open to pillage. He died fighting the Danes for Edmund Ironside at the battle of Assandun in 1016. He was also Ailgifu's grandfather.

Our plan was simple. When Walkelin died, prior knowledge of the first forged charter would be lost. The charter would disappear. The second charter would surface and a claim made for restoration against a deceitful church. With luck and a following wind, Ailgifu or, probably, her eldest son would be made lord of the manor of Alresford which included its three churches and the mead house in Medstead.

We luxuriated in our delayed success.

Our family treasure now exceeded any needs we could foresee in our immediate lifetimes. The coins were split four ways with Lēofric accepting one purse after a short hesitation. Two other purses were buried under the hearths of the mead shop by the fort and of our new house in Ropley.

For all our work on the great survey, the book withered quickly on the vine, uncompleted and unchecked to any great degree and hardly used. It seemed to us that Rufus could not be bothered with the over complex result. While his father wanted to use it to justify an increase in his revenues, Rufus just took any extra he needed. All he needed to do was to unleash Ranulf. At least, a few years later, Samson got his coveted bishopric at Worcester, a peculiar reward for administrative endeavour.

Resources were quickly diverted when, within months, Odo returned to England and raised a rebellion bringing together many of the comrades of the conqueror who held lands in both England and Normandy. The old warriors included Geoffrey de Montbray, met by us at Bentworth, Eustace III, count of Boulogne, son and heir of the Sutton manor holder, and Robert of Mortain, Odo's brother. They wanted to see one manipulable man ruling both the realm and the dukedom. It was a direct challenge to the legitimacy of Rufus and cemented Odo's declaration for Robert Curthose as the rightful ruler. Winchester declared for Rufus although many Norman landowners and northern bishops faded into the background to see how the wind blew.

I moved my family out of the city again and back to Ropley. Lēofric declared that the 'villainous' Odo had to be stopped at any cost. 'Any enemy of Odo is a friend of mine,' he boasted. He temporarily joined the city guard and often arrived home in the early hours of the morning. He received a better sword and scabbard and a new leather jerkin which particularly pleased him. His commitment and martial skills were noticed and applauded by his commander.

Lēofric had all the latest gossip: the king's Easter court was half empty; Odo had five hundred men landed from Normandy, including Eustace III, and proceeded to lay waste to the earldom in Kent, paying particular attention to lands belonging to his old enemy, Lanfranc. Smaller regional uprisings sprung up in Bristol, Bath, Berkeley, Worcestershire, Norfolk, Leicestershire and Northamptonshire. It was a dangerous time. At the end of April, the king called an assembly in Winchester which was backed by the English who saw value in the state standing against the unbridled power of Norman lords and bishops.

The decisive fighting took place in the south east where Odo had based his attack on the castles at Tonbridge, Pevensey and Rochester. Rufus led his men, including Lēofric now in charge of a detachment, and besieged the castles one by one. Odo was starved into submission. He surrendered then changed his mind anticipating a relieving second force from Robert Curthose and fled to Rochester. The force did not come and all was lost.

Lēofric was still excited when he returned. He described two large siege engines. He was among the crowd at the castle gate jeering and demanding that Odo be hanged.

'It was dreadful inside Rochester's walls,' he reported. 'There were men and horses dead from disease and a dreadful plague of flies. I did capture one cup with jewels. Here it is. It was said Odo drank his last wine from it.'

It was a dull affair with some gem sockets empty. It had a significant dent in the base which meant it couldn't stand up. We all eyed it with some disappointment.

'Odo the traitor was let free to our great disgust on the condition that he would leave England and never return unless the king sent for him,' continued Lēofric. 'I guess being an uncle helped. All his lands in England were confiscated as were those of our Eustace. Rufus gave a little speech from his horse and we were all thanked and made a big shout.'

The successful resistance to this third Norman invasion seemed to the English like Lēofric to almost reverse the disaster of 1066.

It was of little surprise to me that Lēofric and I began to drift apart after his adventures. Just as I had become almost English, Lēofric became more Norman. He embraced the martial culture, his appetite for combat whetted by his experiences in Sussex and Kent. Within a year, he was welcomed into the upper echelons of the king's own guard, not a knight, but regarded by all his fellows as worthy of respect and rank.

Ailgifu and I spent time with our family. We rode the boundaries of the old Saxon estates, played with the children and watched them grow. It might have gone on that way forever, but the restless Rufus had other ideas. The king was warmly supported by a council of barons in Winchester in 1090 in a proposal to carry the war across into Normandy. William said that he wanted to avenge himself on his brother, Robert, the duke, and on the treacherous Odo and, in a neat reversal of the argument at the conquest, that he wanted to save the Norman church from the anarchy that prevailed in the duchy. Of course, Lēofric was among the first to volunteer.

The whole escapade was a messy affair of small interest to me. Lēofric reported that there was little fighting, but that he saw a lot of the countryside. I guessed from his later story telling that it was here that he killed his first man or men. Mildgyth complained later that his sleep was always troubled. Except when trying to revitalise his cathedral at Bayeux, Odo was always at Robert's side. A formal treaty was signed at Rouen in February 1091 where Robert agreed to hand over the county of Eu, which Rufus had already occupied, and the abbeys of Fécamp, Mont-Saint-Michel and Cherbourg. Treasure and some English estates changed hands. The most significant part of the treaty was that the king and the duke made each other heir to each other's lands, thus removing from the younger Henry any hope of inheriting either of their titles while one of his brothers lived.

I saw only trouble coming and despaired of the feuds of this Norman family ever ending.

It took almost two years for Lēofric to return home. Messages from him had dried up. He held a senior position, had fifty men at his command, and was one of the first chosen for dangerous missions. Only psychopaths and men looking for glory and treasure would willingly serve with him. We heard he never took prisoners.

I remember like yesterday when, in 1093, he did finally come home. We had just heard that Lanfranc had died. The day before, St Swithun's Day, I stood with Ailgifu and the children watching the monks come from the old minster to the new cathedral carrying the saint's shrine in triumph. The next day, I stood alone as, at Walkelin's bidding, the workmen began to break down the old church. It all came down that year except one porch and the high altar.

I realised that Ranulph Flambard was standing next to me watching the destruction. He was friendly and told me that, with Lanfranc gone, the king had asked him to stay in Winchester and take control of much of his finances.

'William is as welcoming of money as ever his father was,' he offered. 'He has told me to make the king every man's heir be he knight, clerk or layman. There will be heavy burdens on all those not in personal favour. So, we shall be taxing the dead. The king's favourite plan is to keep high positions vacant and to take the revenue or to sell them to the highest bidder. It took three years to replace the abbot of New Minster. It might be years before a new man of sufficient stature is found to hold Canterbury after Lanfranc. And, as for Walkelin, when that wicked man finally leave us, ... who knows.

'You know, Gilbert, I believe that I might become the most hated man in England.'

I felt a nudge in my back, turned, and hardly recognised the gaunt man who stood behind me. He had a face ravaged by memories, hardened by long campaigns. This was a man used to demand respect and for his orders to be executed immediately and without exception. We embraced, but a little stiffly.

'Ranulf,' I said, 'you will remember Lēofric who did much good work for you. He has just returned from fighting for the king in Normandy. He is held in high honour for his deeds.'

I may exaggerate a little to say that Ranulf's jaw dropped, but the change in status and respect was instant. Ranulf nodded and warily welcomed him.

'I have been chasing bishop Odo all across Normandy without success,' Lēofric said. 'I had hoped to end his days. Most recently, I have been restoring order in Rouen after the disturbances there.'

Ranulf excused himself and Lēofric and I watched for a while as the stones fell from the walls.

'That was my home as a young man. All gone now.' Then Lēofric looked at me. 'The young man has gone, too.'

We walked slowly back to the house, stopping several times for him to drink strong ale. He never once asked after Mildgyth or Ailgifu or even the children, not even baby Leo, now a bustling lad. There was no one home. Lēofric found his cot and slept fitfully. I sat in the garden and could hear him calling out as he chased his vivid dreams.

Two days later he came down with a fever. The next day he was covered in spots which grew and broke into foetid sores. Despite the dangers and the abuse, Mildgyth tended him gently for she told me she loved him still. He lost much of his gnarled flesh, his sweats ran like sour rivers without end.

On the fifth day, the fever broke and it seemed likely he would live. One hour, there was celebration and the next, despair. Mildgyth slumped to the floor with a shriek of fear, her hands showing the first of her own pustules. By nightfall, the four children were screaming in their cots. And there they died, one after another, until only a bemused and wasted Andrew remained.

Ailgifu and I had no energy or emotion left. We stared at each other without seeing in a horrified trance. There was nothing left to share, no comfort to give. My clothes were muddy with the graves I dug at night in the churchyard. At least it was hallowed ground, for no priest would permit burials of such polluted bodies. The preferred solution was the flames of hell.

11 THE KING OF JERUSALEM, 1093-1100

The largely completed cathedral announced plans to start its services by Christmas. Before the crowds came, I reflected in the nave with my fourteen-year-old son, Andrew. A few months ago, it seemed that he was on the cusp of turning into a sturdy young man, confident, quick to debate and Saxon-haired. Now, a small boy shrank into my side and held my hand in both of his. His head stayed mostly still while his eyes swivelled around the stark, repetitive and huge cavern in which we sat. I knew he wasn't admiring the constructive boldness of the builders. He was looking to God for his lost friends.

'Is Edith here?' he asked. 'Is she looking after Emma and baby Leo? Can I see them again?'

I clutched him harder and began to sob from within my very soul. I had no easy solution for him for I was living in my own lonely, shocked world. I told him his brother and sisters would always be with him in his heart so he could see them at any time. He didn't understand and thought that both his parents had let him down. Ailgifu, my strong, beautiful Ailgifu, was a husk with dull eyes who barely moved from her chair. I wondered if she would ever return to us. Lēofric was so full of guilt, he seldom came home and when he reeled in he stank of drink and could only mumble a few half words before falling senseless into his cot.

I looked around the new cathedral for comfort, but found none. The new lords of England, strong and resolute, thought the cathedral, abbey and parish churches of their predecessors lacked size and dignity. Many were swept away. Winchester was typical of what I expected of conquerors who were in a hurry to make their mark: grand and monumental, of course, but without a hint of a welcoming soul. Minsters now expressed in stone the dominant ideas of the new masters; they were the centres of Norman rather than English worship.

The four columns of Winchester's six-storey tower landed without ceremony in the middle of the choir. The north transept lacked the ornate and intimate prayerfulness of older churches. It was lit gloomily by lamps and candles with, presumably, paint and metalwork to come later. The few new tombs were distinctive and rigorous. What warmth there was came either from St Swithun's resting place or from the wood stolen from Hempage, already dusty and scarred underfoot, but glowing in the roof of the nave in the winter sun.

Every few minutes, a monk or two would arrive bringing more records and valuables from the minsters, the first two floors of the tower filling with accounts of imperial affairs and ceremonies. Copies of royal, monastic and private wills and charters were placed in this sanctuary while the oldest documents were transferred to the cathedral priory.

It was then that I decided on a whim to take Ailgifu to visit the shrine of St Swithun, her favourite saint, and to pray for a healing. I put the idea to Andrew and he agreed. I was part of the modern belief that did not hold with miracles. I suspect even if I had seen one with my own eyes or touched another with my finger it would have made no difference. But, even for the sceptic, the accounts of miracles were, at least, well-told, dramatic tales. They elicited sympathy for the many unfortunate people, crippled by physical or mental illness, who thought their best hope lay in dragging themselves from shrine to shrine till a saint took pity.

The visit was an undignified affair. Ailgifu was carried to the cathedral in a cart by two paid men while lolling on a stool. At the entrance, I took her in my arms and carried her to the tomb where we sat on the steps. Andrew worked with a cloth to remove spittle and sweat. We prayed. For me, it was the first time since I lived in Bayeux. Nothing happened. I felt empty. There was no sign of recognition on Ailgifu's face. We went slowly home.

And yet, within a week, Ailgifu began to move from her chair to look after her health and hygiene. Perhaps some vestige of faith had penetrated her blankness during the recent visit? By month's end, she could prepare meals in a metronomic fashion. One fortnight, we had the same meal every afternoon, but it was a start. No complaint was made. In the warmer afternoons, she sat facing the garden with Andrew's head on her lap absent-mindedly stroking his fair hair until both fell asleep. I stood nearby, guarding silently.

I taught Andrew to ride and we went all about to Sarum, Southampton, Guildford and even into Kent. We rode mostly without conversation. I pointed out plants, birds, wild animals and special places. He nodded his appreciation, but barely passed a comment. I hardly saw Lēofric, still wracked and unable to talk about my lost children. I knew he had visited by the rumpled, soiled sheets in his room. The chess pieces began to gather dust.

I took the odd job from Ranulf, increasingly distant as his power grew. Ranulf was right. He did become the most hated man in England as he squeezed the finances of every estate he could reach. When Rufus went abroad, it was Ranulf and Walkelin who were appointed as joint regent and both were fully damned by each other's iniquities.

Some two years later, I delivered a long-overdue payment that I had been asked to collect from an unhappy tenant. Ranulf appeared by chance as I was about to leave his outer office. We passed a few cordial minutes and then he suggested I attend an unusual event. Pope Urban's message to the faithful, delivered at Clermont in France, had just been received and was to be read to the Norman nobles and knights of England. The primary concern of Urban, a French pope, was to recruit Frenchmen to his cause.

'I would take your unhappy servant along,' Ranulf suggested.

I had not been back to the cathedral, indeed to any church, since my visit with Ailgifu. Time had largely slipped away.

After some cajoling, I persuaded Lēofric to come with me and, after more encouragement, Andrew as well. The subject of the reading had spread like wildfire. The atmosphere was highly charged; the noise an excited babble. Walkelin and Ranulf, installed on thrones, overlooked a cathedral packed with standing people who spilled into the precinct. A monk with a strong if high pitched voice, shaking in his slippers at such an audience, had been chosen. Walkelin gave a blessing as the din subdued.

The pope enjoined the aristocracy of Christendom to put aside their petty quarrels and set forth to fight the infidel in the east. It was to be a pilgrimage to Jerusalem, a crusade and a holy war. All those who reached the city at the centre of the known world and contributed to its restoration would be granted indulgences for their earthly sins. Others, less concerned for redemption in the afterlife, saw great opportunity for the other preoccupation of Norman and French life: plunder.

From the confines of Jerusalem and the city of Constantinople, a horrible tale has gone forth and very frequently has been brought to our ears, namely, that a race from the kingdom of the Persians, an accursed race, a race utterly alienated from God, a generation forsooth which has not directed its heart and has not entrusted its spirit to God, has invaded the lands of those Christians and has depopulated them by the sword, pillage and fire; it has led away a part of the captives into its own country, and a part it has destroyed by cruel tortures; it has either entirely destroyed the churches of God or appropriated them for the rites of its own religion. They destroy the altars, after having defiled them with their uncleanness. They circumcise the Christians, and the blood of the circumcision they either spread upon the altars or pour into the vases of the baptismal font ...

What shall I say of the abominable rape of the women? To speak of it is worse than to be silent.

The kingdom of the Greeks is now dismembered by them and deprived of territory so vast in extent that it can not be traversed in a march of two months.

On whom therefore is the labour of avenging these wrongs and of recovering this territory incumbent, if not upon you?[1] You, upon whom above other nations God has conferred remarkable glory in arms, great courage, bodily activity, and strength to humble the hairy scalp of those who resist you.

Let the deeds of your ancestors move you and incite your minds to manly achievements ... who have destroyed the kingdoms of the pagans, and have extended in these lands the territory of the holy church. Let the holy sepulchre of the Lord our Saviour, which is possessed by unclean nations, especially incite you, and the holy places which are now treated with ignominy and irreverently polluted with their filthiness.

Oh, most valiant soldiers and descendants of invincible ancestors, be not degenerate, but recall the valour of your progenitors.

There was a great roar and commitments filled the church to the roof where they stayed until practical matters like financing and the safeguarding of home manors brought many down to earth. The very building smelled of the sweat

---

1   French-speaking nobles.

of battle. Lēofric raised both his arms and saw immediately a path that would release him from his great despair. I knew no argument would dissuade him. I took some hours to restrain Andrew for whom this was a first encounter with religious fervour. In the end, I had to forbid him signing his name.

Many powerful men from the Frankish world rose to prepare for the pilgrimage willing to leave behind their castles and cities, their wives and children and their great estates. Dead William's eldest son, Robert Curthose, duke of Normandy, financed his retinue with a mortgage of 10,000 silver marks from his brother, William Rufus, in return for five years of control of Normandy. Rufus raised the money by stripping English churches of their jewels and by a tax of four shillings on the hide, collected rigorously by Ranulf's men with me occasionally in tow. The king went in person to Rouen to deliver the sixty-seven barrels of bullion coin and to take possession of his temporary dukedom.

Odo attended the council in Clermont as Curthose's emissary. Ironically, he also had a private meeting with the pope after which he stirred his aged bones and joined Robert on the crusade. With Rufus in charge, Normandy was not a place for Odo to stay. Breton Ralph de Gael, once earl of East Anglia, and his wife Emma, banished to Brittany, and count Eustace III of Boulogne, whose father was at one time lord of the manor of Sutton, were prominent.

The crusade's great departure was to be around August the following year under orders given by pope Urban. Walkelin used the turmoil to lessen the financial burden of the new cathedral. In a coup sufficient to drive Ranulf into a spectacular outburst of rage, Rufus granted the bishop and his monks a licence for a three-day, annual fair on St Giles Hill. To Ranulf's spitting disgust, Rufus added all his personal rents in the city for the period. The fair was an immediate international success and brought much foreign trade and many strange merchants to Winchester. While it was open, it entirely superseded all local businesses, shops and stalls and, for seven leagues around, closed premises even as far as Alton and Southampton. To rub in his victory over Ranulf, Walkelin asked me to make the arrangements for the diversion of rents.

War is an expensive occupation, even more so in a foreign land. A properly equipped half-knight like Lēofric, with no armour, arms, war-horses, pack-horses or servants, had to plan for a costly journey. To travel without sponsorship was not an option, but richer men could bring the poorer into their service. Money and supplies received by fair means or foul along the way would not plug the gap. What made it worse was that Lēofric would not sign for any 'traitorous' Norman.

We agreed a part compromise. It involved digging up one of our buried purses and putting the whole of it to Lēofric's personal horse, armour and equipment. In return, he promised to send word when he had found a lord. He left for France in the middle of 1096 carrying with him letters of recommendation from the Norman knights in the royal guard in Winchester whom he so despised. I committed that, if he did not return, I would make an endowment on the church at Medstead so that his soul would always rest in the soil of Wessex. He spent his last day in Winchester like a true knight, prostrate in prayer by our little plot of graves in St Michael's churchyard. Next morning, Andrew stood with me as Lēofric made his lonely way down the High Street towards the East Gate.

[*Editor's note: Lēofric wrote three letters while on pilgrimage, three years between the first and the last. They were all found within the folds of Gilbert's manuscript; the only writings not in Gilbert's hand. Extracts have been brought together for literary convenience.*]

Good news! The tyrant Odo of Bayeux is dead! We are wintering with Norman families in Apulia and Calabria. Odo joined our party although I kept away from him even while planning his last days from a distance. He visited Robert the Great, Norman count of Sicily, in Palermo, died there, and is buried in the cathedral. I wept no tears. My only sadness was that his death was not by my hand.

When I arrived in France, I went straight to visit countess Ida of Boulogne, the widow for nine years of Eustace II. I told her I was from her husband's manor of Sutton in England and I wished to pilgrimage. She was delighted with the recommendations that I gave her. Her three sons, Eustace III, Godfrey and Baldwin are to go to Jerusalem and I am to join them. The sons declare they are seized by hope of an eternal inheritance and by love of God in the fight for Jerusalem. They have sold or relinquished all their possessions to fund the journey. Ida has made an endowment to the abbey of St Bertin for all our safeties. She is highly religious and corresponds regularly with our new Anselm who waits at Canterbury.

The crusade is wildly popular in France with the peasantry and nobles alike. It has become a divine enterprise. Liberation is the word most commonly used: first to free the eastern churches in general and the church of Jerusalem in particular from the ravages of the Muslims; second to free the city of Jerusalem. Of course, Urban means to make this a liberation under the papal banner. He asked the regional priests, those he charged with local organisation, why the pilgrimage was so popular? The answer was split between love of God and love of Mammon.

Another reason is that the preaching of Urban's crusade coincided with outbreaks of ergotism, something we in England see little. It is an unpleasant disease caused by eating bread made from mouldy rye. These epidemics are common in France and often result in mass pilgrimages which seek to alleviate distress.

* * * *

We were in the second wave of crusaders and left Apulia in late August. Even during preparation for invasion, individual pilgrim parties were travelling to Jerusalem unmolested. We headed for Constantinople and I have much enjoyed the place. In April, we all came together before the city of Nicaea. There was a great siege. I have been given a captaincy under the third brother, Baldwin, and am grateful for their sponsorship and supply of goods. My horse died in battle, but, in truth, he had grown too weak. We are now to march across Asia Minor.

There have been some bad times. The early leavers, in June and July, saw no difference between slaughtering the Jews in Europe and attacking the Muslims in the East. Both are enemies of the faith. The Norman crusaders in south Italy held Jews, heretics and Muslins as equally detestable. It was seen as unjust for those who took up arms against rebels against Christ to allow enemies of Christ to live in their own land. I am told that the Jews are more hostile to God than any other race and revenge was desired on them for the crucifixion. The Jewish community at Mainz was annihilated; in June those Jews in Cologne were hunted and destroyed. The massacres continued in Trier and in Metz. I pity for the Jews in Winchester and England if this madness takes hold there.

Urban has introduced the cross as a symbol to be sewn on the crusader's clothing. I have led the way with my men who all now have a large red cross on a white background on their outer tunics.

* * * *

This may be my last letter. I am too weak to write and I dictate what I can, slowly, to a priest who is tending us. We are on a ship bound for the French coast. The heat below decks is awful. The arrow wound in my back has turned bad and I am encouraged to spend all my time praying to God. All my sins are forgiven because I reached Jerusalem with Godfrey and Baldwin and was in the first party to enter the city. There are only a hundred knights left there now as many are returning home, duty done and oath fulfilled.

Baldwin and Godfrey broke away from the main army to raid Cilicia, and we took Tarsus, Adana, Misis and Edessa. We then went through a devastating wilderness in central Anatolia where horses and pack animals died like flies. Much of the time, we were out of contact with Christian suppliers. We needed cash and looted the countryside and despoiled every army and town we took.

We marched down the Palestine coast and then inland to Jerusalem. We passed through narrow gaps between sea and mountains, passages that could be closed by a small defending force. It was a risk. Local rulers hastened to make peace, pay tribute and open their markets.

We arrived at Jerusalem in May. On a midday in July, I was with Godfrey on a siege tower that we had pushed against the city's curtain wall. We used vinegar to put out flammable missiles akin to Greek fire. Close by, a defensive tower caught fire and was evacuated. Godfrey cut loose a hide-covered wattle protecting us and fashioned a makeshift bridge across to the ramparts.

Your Lēofric of Winchester was with Godfrey in the leading party into the Holy City! Do you think I will be remembered in the cathedral? The Muslim defence collapsed immediately. There was great slaughter.

I received my arrow at a great battle at Ascalon, a port near the city where a Fatimid army had come to dispossess us.[2] We were less than half their men. We charged at dawn through sleeping guards and put over 10,000 to the sword.

We heard a mass for Lēofric in July in the year 1100 after we received his last missive. A separate letter arrived at the same time with news of his death. Nothing official could be arranged, explained the bureaucrats, because Lēofric was not a Norman and there was great jealousy over his deeds. Our private affair in the cathedral was well attended by Ailgifu's family from Medstead and several hundred monks with heritage in the city's minsters. A simple plaque was quietly placed by friends in the nave close to Walkelin's tomb. Other news arrived much later in the year: Eustace III had returned to France and entered a monastery. His brother, Godfrey of Bouillon, had declined the title of king of Jerusalem as no crown of jewels was appropriate in the city of the crown of thorns. He died within twelve months. The youngest brother, Baldwin, however, did take the title. I wondered whether the family of the king of Jerusalem still held the manor of Sutton in any guise? Everything, as always, was claimed by the church.

Walkelin's death seemed like a direct punishment for his complicity. The king had ordered him to transfer two hundred marks without delay and Walkelin saw that without squeezing the poor or robbing churches yet again, no such sum could be paid. He grew weary of life and prayed to God to be released and was dead ten days later. He was buried before the steps under the screen that divides the nave from the choir in which stands the silver cross of Stigand.

Walkelin lies buried beneath here, cathedral-builder in the time of William the Conqueror
Also Lēofric of Winchester, conqueror of Jerusalem with Godfrey of Bouillon, Defender of the Holy Sepulchre, mortally wounded at Ascalon, buried at sea

I think Lēofric had the last and best word. When the surprisingly large group of mourners had left, I sat alone with Ailgifu and Andrew. It was our first outing

---

2   Fatimid: An Ismaili Shia caliphate which lasted from the tenth to the twelfth centuries, spanning a large area of North Africa from the Atlantic Ocean to the Red Sea.

together since that dreadful day. I cried properly for the first time for my lost children. I also cried for myself. The confirmation of the death of my oldest and best friend meant I was nearing my own time. My bones were beginning to ache. I prayed fervently that Ailgifu would continue her recovery and that she and Andrew and I would have some happiness.

At Walkelin's death, Lanfranc was finally replaced at Canterbury by Anselm, the second greatest churchman and intellectual of my time. Both men came to England from south of the Alps. They separately built up the monastery at Bec into one of the most famous and enterprising schools in Europe and became in succession archbishops of Canterbury. Ranulf loved to tell me that, although Anselm was accustomed to worldly business, he refused to intrigue, but discoursed on the scriptures instead. If no one listened, he would go to sleep, but when he woke he would demolish his opponents' arguments in a moment. Not surprisingly, after disputes with Rufus, he was sent into exile.

There was another great ecclesiastical change which took my breath away. In 1099, Ranulf Flambard, the brightest of men and sharpest of crooks, paid £1,000 to gain the bishopric of Durham. This was a man who continued to visit Winchester to 'skin the rich, grind down the poor and sweep other men's inheritances into the king's net'. Ranulf venerated and feared St Cuthbert whose sanctuary he rebuilt in Durham and from which he removed without hesitation any criminal who sought asylum.

The month after Lēofric's cathedral mass, William Rufus was brought into the city dripping with gore in a crazy two-wheeled cart of a charcoal burner drawn, I thought, by a sorry nag. He was another victim of his family's devotion to hunting. He died like his older brother, Richard, in the New Forest, one of the royal forests which covered about a quarter of the country. The forests gave each king revenue and recreation as well as jurisdiction over dangerous terrain. They were also the refuge of patriots and outlaws, like in Chawton and Waltham.

I pieced together what happened. There were many similarities to the royal clan's other deaths in England.

The hunting party set off late rather than at first light as was customary. After a dinner, the men's reaction times were perhaps dulled. Low evening sun shone into the eyes of some of the archers. Rufus shot an arrow and wounded a stag which ran off. Sir Walter Tirel, a French baron, shot at another stag. The arrow glanced off an animal or a tree and pierced the king's heart, but I also hear tell that the king was left unconscious and speechless before he died. Tirel declared the death was a complete accident, but quickly fled the scene. He rode to the coast, took ship to France and never returned. Ranulf told me that he decided there would be no investigation unless one was called for. Nobody asked.

Henry, the youngest brother, moved quickly. He rode immediately to Winchester, arriving before the body, and took control of the royal treasury marking his claim to the throne. The following day, I attended in the background as Rufus was buried in the New Minster with proper but brief ceremonial. The Royal Council met at the shortest notice. Many of the nobles still wished for Robert Curthose to succeed, but the duke was thought to be in southern Italy and his friends were not strong enough to delay the election. There were fiery arguments. Henry claimed he had the right to rule because his parents had been king and queen at his birth which was not the case with Robert. The English cabal won the day and Henry, the English-born, English-speaking prince, became the candidate of the political establishment. The party of the king elect rode quickly to London and Henry was crowned in Westminster Abbey just three days after Rufus had died.

Like everyone else, I was caught up in the conspiracy theories. I joined the crowds jostling for news but, for the first time, I had no Lēofric with inside information or his particular pithy and cynical interpretation of events.

How had Henry arrived in Winchester so quickly after the death? It was certain that he was hunting in the forest at the same time. Perhaps Henry acted immediately to forestall a rapid return by his elder brother from the crusade? How was the Council so quickly formed? The treasury opened and claimed? The coronation organised? Did Tirel really make the bowshot? Why did he run? How would a glancing arrow pierce a heart? Who apart from Henry benefitted? Was an order for regicide quietly given?

Above all, Henry was acknowledged by all who knew him as a proven, cold-hearted murderer. Many years ago, before Rufus's death, Conan Pilatus, a powerful Rouen burgher, sided with Rufus against Robert in the never-ending fraternal war in Normandy. Henry entered the fray on Robert's side, took Conan prisoner, dragged him to the battlements of Rouen Castle and threw him off.

Without delay, Henry conferred the see of Winchester left vacant by Walkelin on William Giffard, a previous dean of Rouen, who had been Rufus's chancellor.

Henry called Anselm home to Canterbury, but via Wissant in the county of Boulogne to avoid enemies in Normandy. He then dismissed Ranulf and sent him to the newly completed prison at the Tower of London. Ranulf was the obvious scapegoat for all the financial extortions of Rufus's reign.

Henry's coronation charter was sent to every shire as soon as his seal was ready. A copy was nailed to the New Minster door in Winchester. The charter sought to capture the loyalty of any possible opposition. All men of rank were required to give an oath that they would defend the realm especially against his brother Robert of Normandy. Henry offered to free the church, give more latitude to his barons, abolish all unjust transactions left by Rufus and Ranulf, to be a good lord, to limit his own powers especially in marriage and inheritance and in the contribution that must be made to him through taxation.

Henry's bride in November that year was Edith, the daughter of Malcolm III, king of the Scots, and Margaret. She was educated in part at the nunnery at Wilton. In a curious way, this marriage rejoined the Norman dynasty to the House of Wessex. It is worth the diversion. When, in 1016, king Edmund Ironside died and Cnut, by arrangement, became sole ruler of England, Edmund's two sons fled to Hungary. One of them married a Hungarian wife and their children later returned to England as the sole survivors of the old English royal family. Two of these children had names, Margaret and Christina, which at that time were unknown in England, but became popular. Margaret married Malcolm of Scotland and her daughter, Edith, given the royal name of Matilda, married Henry.

Lēofric would have enjoyed greatly discrediting this story of the reconnecting of the royal houses.

It was obvious to me that times had changed for ever. With his desperate coronation charter, Henry had forgone significant monies. In time past, Ranulf would have called me to the Winchester treasury to help find imaginative places from which to squeeze new revenue. To compensate for his loss, Henry had to exploit the crown's rights over farms, feudal dues, profits of justice and incomes from vacant churches. This would all require detailed and continuous records. The *Winchester Book*, almost twenty years out of date, quickly became inadequate. In truth, it was out of date and adulterated before it was finished. New records had to be made and kept from year to year. Previously unnoticed barons arrived from Normandy and took prominent positions. The empty bishoprics were filled.

The word was that Henry's new men who he 'raised from the dust' were all Normans with little experience of England.

It was also obvious to me that Winchester's role as the centre of England was coming to a slow end. For so long as the English king was also duke of Normandy, Winchester lay handiest for Rouen. The connection was now regularly broken. Chests of documents frequently travelled up and down to London. The new great men preferred to live elsewhere. The importance of the southern capital began to wane.

Why did I muse on these things? It is simple. During all this upheaval, no one called for my services. My time of usefulness had ended. I was also cruelly alone. Andrew yearned for a life away from our house and its memories. At least he did ask my permission before he moved to Ropley and began to care for the bees. He could start to breathe again in the open spaces on the ridge and he felt more at home with his Saxon family in Medstead. With time to think, he could make up his mind about another decision. He was considering becoming a monk in order to spend his life steeped in religion and learning. I made sure that he had enough pennies to order supplies of his few delicacies in Alresford.

Although he would never say it, Andrew was also pleased to be away from the constant drain of helping to care for Ailgifu. The long hoped for recovery never came. The eyes remained dull, the small enthusiasms always absent, company or religion never requested, recognition coupled with a thank you almost never present. She had the best of care and most interesting of diets, but she never noticed. When she did speak, she was often incoherent and never touched matters at hand. Her mind was entrapped or elsewhere.

Ailgifu and I spent the loneliest Christmas festive season together. After I had washed her, placed her in her cot, prayed over her, I would often sit long into the night, drink in hand, and wonder why God was punishing me. Of course, every hour I missed all my children. And Lēofric. Always Lēofric.

One early morning in February, I neither knew nor cared which, I was awakened well before dawn by a heavy banging on the door. I half dressed and found a dozen men-at-arms outside, none known to me. I was under arrest on the orders of the king, suspected of high treason and to be taken for interrogation.

After some aggressive arguing, I was allow to dress appropriately, walk a few paces to waken one of the women in the same street who helped me care for Ailgifu and to ask her to send a message to Andrew in case I never returned.

I was bundled unkindly into the back of a noisome straw cart. I was not allowed a horse for fear of an attempted escape. We trundled out of Winchester into the still dark night.

12 ALTON'S CLOTH OF GOLD, 1101-1112

The cart wheels left the mud track and rattled over crushed stones leading to what I found to be a long barn. After a brief, muffled exchange, my guard rode back to the city. The awning was lifted and, to my surprise, an arm offered as I climbed down. I was glad of the help because my legs were stiff with cold. I caught a glimpse of the ruins of the Roman aqueduct which took water to the centre of Winchester. The first light of the sun did little to break through the rain. The river mist hid what I knew to be the Itchen. I heard the sharp splashing of drops in puddles, the occasional whinnying of horses in a nearby stable, the murmur of men talking softly. Four guards rubbed their hands over the embers of a log fire, their crossbows propped close at hand. A serjeant-at-arms came forward.

'Master Gilbert,' he said. 'I am sorry to see you here. I know you as the good friend of Lēofric of Jerusalem. Would you had chosen all your friends as carefully. I am forbidden to answer your questions. Please follow me.'

I was led into the house. To my left, I caught sight of loaves and large cuts of fresh meat on the kitchen table. I was taken right, past the stairs, through the hall still warm from last night's meals and into a parlour. A poor candle was lit and it smoked blackly. A servant brought weak wine, some crusts, the remains of a cold pigeon pie and an apple. The serjeant indicated a bench. I sat, ate, waited and worried about myself, but mostly about Ailgifu. This was not the sort of interrogation I had anticipated.

After an hour, which was filled with impressive snoring from overhead, I heard movement in the chambers and the enthusiastic use of several piss pots. Men stomped down the stairs and occupied one of the tables in the hall. Food was brought. There was purposeful conversation, but too low to decipher. Chairs were rearranged and I caught the rustling of parchment. The serjeant came back to my parlour.

'Time,' was all he said.

At one end of a long trestle, two men sat facing me. Both picked at several plates of leftovers. Their goblets were full. Nearby, a scribe perched, quill poised. I did not recognise any of them, but they were well dressed if a little dishevelled. I heard a scraping noise and saw that there was a fourth man, his chair rocking on two legs, leaning against the far wall in the quarter light.

'You are Gilbert of Bayeux?'

'I am, but once of Bayeux. I am now of Winchester and Ropley. May I ask who you are?'

'I am Geoffrey Ridel and sitting beside me is Ralph Basset. Do you know who we are?'

'I know you are both men of the king and sometimes hold court for him. I know you both from the *Winchester Book*. You have lands in Northamptonshire. From your accent, you are a Norman from Sicily. Ralph Basset is a Norman who has land in Buckinghamshire and Hertfordshire.'

'You are very well informed, Gilbert. Do you know why you are here?'

'I was told by armed men that I was arrested on suspicion of treason against the king.'

'And, what do you say to this charge?'

'I reject it absolutely. I have never, and would never, plot against the lawful king. I was servant to Odo, bishop of Bayeux, for near twenty years and have worked for another thirty for two kings of England through their appointed officers. I was a clerk and a messenger. No criticism of my conduct has ever been put to me. Besides, I have turned away from power. I have no ambition in that regard.'

'Have you ever stolen from the king?'

'Again, never. I am not poor, but I am not rich. I rent my house in Winchester from the prior. I have a humble house in Ropley where my sick wife and I keep bees and make honey. We have a mead house in Medstead which is managed by my wife's brothers.'

'Do you think Odo was a good choice as master?'

'I did not choose my Lord. I was an orphan and he took me into his kitchens. He was grateful to me for several services. When I knew him best, he was working to build the armada and, later, to protect king William and to reform the church.'

'Do you think Ranulf Flambard was a good choice of master?'

Here we were getting close to the point, I thought.

'Ranulf excelled at raising taxes at the king's request. He was also avaricious and he could be vicious. He had a lot to recommend him, but he needed to be watched and understood by his own masters. Because of my paid services through him to William Rufus, I no longer have employment.'

I was then questioned closely about the last time I had met Ranulf.

'Do you know where Ranulf is today?'

I explained that I heard he had been charged with embezzlement of the royal finances. He was the first prisoner in William's great castle tower in London. There was a pause which I filled.

'May I suggest, with great respect, that you tell me what is going on. I cannot help you best if I do not know.'

There was a longer pause; then a cough from the back of the room. I got my explanation from Ridel.

Ranulf had escaped from the tower of London. Friends had a flagon of wine taken to his cell. The wine was given to the guards who, when drunk, fell asleep. The flagon also contained a rope which Ranulf used to climb down from a window. A ship waited with some of the bishop's treasure and his elderly mother. The next day he was in Normandy and took refuge at the court of Robert Curthose, the duke.

There followed the longest pause yet.

'What do you say to that, Gilbert of many places?'

I shrugged. I was amused at Ranulf, given to fat in middle age, dangling from a rope.

'We are stripping Ranulf of his lands. Gerard of York will depose him of his bishopric. Will you be following Ranulf to Normandy? Or do you have tasks from him here in England?'

I gave a just audible and deliberate chuckle. This was the make or break moment. I had to appear confident and, therefore, unafraid.

'Before you answer,' said Ridel, 'you should know that Ranulf's custodian, William de Mandeville, is now painfully held for his connivance in the escape. You will also know that Mandeville is the son-in-law of Eudo Dapifer another of your friends through his brother Adam who is lately dead. The dapifer now holds the tower for the king.'

I said that much of this information was new to me. I grieved for Adam as a true friend. I had not heard from Ranulf, did not know he was in Normandy and would certainly, on my oath, not be going there. I thought it bad news for the king's security that these events had happened.

'How so?' charged Basset with alacrity.

'In my view, Ranulf will already be at the duke's ear,' I explained. 'He is a man with a silver tongue. He will stiffen Robert's sinews. He has the capacity to bring wishful thinking into being. He is capable of organising an invasion fleet. I suspect he will not be long in pushing Robert to action. I suspect that you will not be able to stop this except by battle or by treaty.'

The man in the background dropped his chair onto its four legs. He spoke for the first time.

'What is to be offered by us in a treaty?'

'If Ranulf is the energy behind the duke's new conviction, your Highness, then he is equally the man who can undermine it. If battle is not joined, then the negotiations must take place in three parts: the first between you and your brother; the second between the lords and nobles; and the third quietly with Ranulf and people who know him best. Ranulf would welcome forgiveness and the return of his bishopric. Ranulf could then persuade your brother to accept a cash pension and the whole of Normandy. Once the danger is past, both men can be kept apart for ever.'

'And, then ...?'

'And then deal with both men separately at a later time at your convenience.'

'You are suggesting that I invade Normandy after making the treaty?'

'Yes, Sire, but only when you decide it is necessary and that you will win. It will not be the first war between the sons of the Conqueror. It will also flush out any of your enemies who remain hidden.'

I was eyed up and down.

'You are most forthright and a confident counsellor, Gilbert,' said Basset.

Henry made his decision.

'My men will come for you, Gilbert, if my brother and Ranulf do invade. I expect you to be at my side to do your loyal duty.'

I was given a fine horse, mine to keep, a comfortable purse for my trouble, and an escort back to Winchester. It was a far cry from my journey in the other direction just a few hours before. I was met at the door by a distraught Andrew. I thought he was concerned for my safety. I couldn't have been more wrong.

'Where have you been?' he shouted. 'How could you leave mother like this? You may be too late.'

Ailgifu had wakened and tried to find me in the dark house, constantly calling my name as she wandered. The neighbour tried to calm her. When Andrew arrived, she had fallen into a kind of trance, staring blankly at my cot.

I cradled her head and kissed her. After a few moments, she opened her eyes and looked blankly at me.

'Where is my Gilbert?' she asked. 'Where is my Edith?'

She gave a little cough and slipped away to peace.

Andrew sobbed without restraint for his mother and, I believe, finally, for all his siblings and for Lēofric and Mildgyth.

'Where were you?' he accused. 'What could have been more important than being here with her at the end?'

Rumours about Robert's impending invasion fleet grew steadily and became wilder by the day. Many landowners left the city for the countryside security of their manors. Ailgifu was buried first in the churchyard at Medstead in a shallow grave. I placed a small plaque on the wall on the cramped nave. So many people attended that her mead shop by the castle ran dry. Andrew stayed for three days in prayer and then moved to New Minster. A week later, he and I returned with a stone coffin with a heavy top. Ailgifu's body fitted neatly and we took it by wagon to the hillside between Medstead and Ropley and laid her in the ground. I said the Saxon rites. From her last home, she was able to watch over her bees.

I set about finding what I could about my new Lord, the king of England. I was told Henry was not a creature of institutions. He believed in men of ability. From the ranks, he raised skilled men who paid great attention to detail and made them formidable even to the greatest barons of the kingdom. Geoffrey Ridel and Ralph Basset were typical of the type. Another was Robert, bishop of Salisbury, his domestic manager and chancellor. It was said Robert endeared himself to the king by the speed at which he said mass. It made him the ideal priest for military men.

The court, alongside the new school at Oxford, was the university of the day. Henry was a man who knew how to run a complex organisation. Mornings were devoted to business. Experienced counsellors sat alongside the king and formal discussions often extended into dinner. The reign was full of novelties: the first royal financial accounts, the first charter of liberties, the first foreign treaty.

Henry repeatedly said that he wished his greatest glory would be the peace of his kingdom and the prosperity of his subjects. After an afternoon sleep, there was time for the young to indulge in more pleasurable pursuits. The king's court in the forenoon was a school of virtues and wisdom and in the afternoon one of hilarity and decent mirth.

Henry could also be a cruel man. To fall foul of him was often fatal.

It was only a few months before unhappy Norman lords, mostly remnants of the Conqueror's time, invited Robert Curthose to England. He assembled his fleet of two hundred ships at Tréport, the fourth Norman invasion of England. They were met by an English flotilla sent by Henry which promptly changed allegiance. Landing at Portsmouth, Robert met the dissatisfied Norman barons at Portchester Castle. His army swelled to three thousand men under the joint command of Ranulf.

At Winchester, I narrowly missed being trapped within the walls. Robert heard that queen Matilda was lying in with her first child in the castle. He marched past the city towards London with some supposed gallantry so as not to disturb her. However, being caught by a chasing army while laying siege was also not a good choice. Robert and his large force travelled through Alresford, Medstead and the woods of Chawton before arriving at the source of the Wey by Alton.

Henry had called out his levies from the shires, made everyone swear an oath of loyalty and camped at a road junction at Wartling, guarding the roads to Pevensey and Hastings. He was outmanoeuvred by the landing at Portsmouth and had to dash up the Meon valley to intercept his brother.

I was scooped up in the night without notice by my guard and we rode hard for an hour. Henry faced the invaders and rebels on open ground between Chawton and Alton. I watched impressed as the king moved through the ranks encouraging his soldiers and giving them instructions in military tactics, especially against Robert's superior cavalry. Many Norman barons acted entirely in their own interests, making demands and switching to Robert when they were refused. To others, Henry followed my advice, and made promises to be paid in the future. The king was outnumbered three to two.

Robert, the oldest son, rode into the neutral ground and challenged Henry, the youngest, to a personal trial of arms unless he gave up the throne.

I had never been at the scene of a battle and watched in amazement at the organisation of the cavalry, the archers and the foot soldiers. The din was all about: from excited horses, shouted orders, taunting screams of bravado and the responses, the clangs of metal, the thump of marching feet. Five thousand men bathed in a sea of colour all within view of each other and framed by the wood, low hills and houses.

The sun was rising. It would be a hot August day. This battle at Alton could change the course of English history.

I suspected that Robert's challenge to hand-to-hand combat was hollow. For brother to fight brother to the death in such a public way was not likely. In truth, family connections through blood and marriage littered and joined both sides. This conflict was about naked power. Three knights, Robert de Bellême, William of Mortain and Eustace of Boulogne, came forward from Robert's side. In a masterstroke, archbishop Anselm led Robert of Meulan and Richard de Redvers in response; that the head of the church in England stood by the king had a visible and sobering effect on the rebels.

After a brief discourse, it was agreed to negotiate. The decision ripped though the field like a pierced bladder. The tension of imminent bloodshed dissipated. Horsemen dismounted, weapons were stacked, food prepared, friends across the lines recognised and greeted. Two large tents of coloured silk were brought forward and filled with facing benches. The brothers entered one with their immediate entourage; the most prominent barons paraded to the other.

This was my time to act. I trotted forward with Eudo Dapifer to where Ranulf sat deciding how to play his hand.

'Good heavens, Gilbert, are you for the usurper king? I did not expect you to prosper from my imprisonment. And, you here, too, Eudo. To what purpose do we meet?'

'My Lord, the king, has suggested that we might usefully talk. The subject of your bishopric at Durham was mentioned.'

'Gilbert, you listened well when you worked for me. I agree. Let us three talk.'

We made for a smaller tent set up some discreet distance away for our use. Our negotiations were, in fact, concluded quickly. Ranulf recognised that, unless Henry was killed in battle, he would never be able to reclaim Durham and the tomb of his beloved St Cuthbert. The cancellation of this dispossession was his principal objective. In return, Ranulf would advise Robert to accept a brotherly compromise: Normandy in its entirety, for Robert, England and the crown without exception for Henry. Robert would renounce his claim to the throne in return for a sum of money, later set by others at 3,000 pounds of silver a year, about a tenth of the royal income. To save face for Robert, we suggested that when the first of Robert and Henry died, the survivor would become heir to all England and Normandy 'unless the deceased had an heir in lawful wedlock'. Of course, everyone was to be forgiven for their part in the affair as long as they chose one side and relinquished their lands in the other. Eustace of Boulogne, brother to the king of Jerusalem, was the only one to be mentioned in the treaty as his extensive loss of lands from his previous rebellion were recognised and returned, including his land at Sutton.

I knew Henry would enjoy deciding whether to settle his grievances later with those who stood against him, but wished to remain in England.

'How will you persuade Robert to accept?' I asked.

'I think it will be easy,' said Ranulf. 'He does not want to kill his remaining brother, an anointed king. The power of the church, through Anselm, is deep within him. He is scarred by his time in the Holy Land and the slaughter he saw. He went there, in part, because the pope called for an end to the eternal wars between the Norman brotherhood. He believes he will be secure if he rules all the old dukedom, especially if Henry has his back.'

We returned to Winchester and I got out my quill with Ranulf at my side. There were many iterations, but the treaty was signed by twelve men on either side on 2 August, a year exactly since Rufus died. Ranulf returned quietly to Normandy to await the papers that re-established him at Durham.

While in the writing room, I found time to place the second charter from so long ago among the papers of the manor of Alresford. It was, perhaps, a pointless gesture. What did it matter to me now whether Alresford and Medstead remained a stolen part of the Winchester bishopric? One day, someone might find it and free the local people.

I was unprepared for the level of my king's gratitude. A week later, I was called to the castle and, without ceremony, and despite my protestation, knighted. I was given a life pension and a large purse. I was offered a manor, but declined, asking only that my land at Ropley continued without hindrance.

As for any other gifts, I asked for two approvals. First, the royal recommendation with a financial gift, to support my son's entry into a teaching monastery. I had discussed the options with Andrew: Winchester, Colchester which Eudo had made his special project, even Durham with a grateful Ranulf, but Andrew's wish was for Anselm and Canterbury and it was granted. Second, I reminded Henry that his father had prohibited the sale of any man outside the country. I said I had heard that both Anselm and Wulfstan, bishop of Worcester, had asked him to complete the work by outlawing the slave trade in England as unbefitting a Norman realm under God. Next year, the council of Westminster promulgated that 'no one is henceforth to be sold like brute beasts'. It was my proudest moment. I hoped Ailgifu would agree.

The council also acted to clean up the church of its sins that I knew so well: the purchase of church offices, stopping clerical marriages, sodomy and drunkenness, and standards of clerical appearance with hair cut short so that a part of the ear and the eyes should be visible.

Henry was not especially partial to honey so I had nothing extra or special to offer in return.

'I know that you wish to stay away from the mainstream of royal affairs,' concluded Henry. 'I shall miss your advice as you return to your bees. However, I have a project that will provide you with additional interest? It might appeal?'

What could I say? It was to be my last major work.

'As you know, the listing of lands in the *Winchester Book* did not include the cities of Winchester and London,' he explained. 'I wish to recover those royal rights in Winchester which king Edward enjoyed. I have ordered your bishop, William Giffard, and four lay courtiers and commissioners to put the burgesses on oath and to make enquiry into the matter. It will be a list of all the city's royal lands which paid rents for the burgage plots and houses and the licences to brew ale. I want you to be one of the courtiers.'

Ralph Basset and Geoffrey Ridel were also appointed as commissioners and, when we met a few months later to begin our plans, it made for an interesting recall of our first meeting by the Itchen. The two other men closely associated with the royal treasury, Herbert the chamberlain, and William of Pont de l'Arche had local connections and knowledge, but not as deep as mine. I found all these men honest and able. The king clearly held them in high regard. They were chosen for their integrity as judges and against the power of bullies. Basset showed me his new seal: a man naked in the jaws of a griffin and being rescued by an armed knight whose blow needed to be carefully calibrated. He wished to draw attention to his role as a protector of the weak.

The commissioners told me that Robert had finally left England, a diminished figure, they thought. He had waited only for the harvest to be gathered and his pension to be paid.

This was a sworn inquisition. We listened attentively as eighty-six of the most prominent burgesses of Winchester listed the royal lands in the city and the rents due from them. Our itinerary was straightforward: first the High Street then the northern side-streets from west to east followed by the south east to west. I think we did good work.

I spent my time over the next years in solitary pursuits. The bees took up most time and their honey became sought after in the towns around. Few visited. Twice a year, I rode to Canterbury to see Andrew and, the first time, I gave him Lēofric's chess board and pieces, hoping he would gain some of the pleasure it once gave me. Keeping it had proved a painful reminder. My favourite local rides took me past the Saxon boundaries where I occasionally met shepherds and drovers and heard their gossip. I always ended on the hill above Eacges gate on the royal road. I could talk to Ailgifu through the hours. On very bad days, I went to the mead shop in Medstead and drank too much to ride home.

King Henry spent his time with revenge in mind. He inflicted severe penalties on those who stood against him during the invasion. New crimes were found, not covered by the Alton treaty. One by one, the rebel barons were displaced. Finally, he turned to the most powerful, Robert of Bellême, accusing him of forty-five offences. Robert's castles at Arundel, Tickhill, Shrewsbury and Bridgnorth fell and he agreed to perpetual banishment. Henry's court trundled around the country. His daily needs, Ridel told me, included wine, pepper, cumin, ginger, towels with a washbasin, herrings, unguents, oil and nuts. He requisitioned local mills for baking. A visit of a few days could bankrupt a host. It was said that he tried to put a curb on the court's excesses, but he set the tone by sleeping with many women 'for the love of begetting children'. Henry was so frightened of plots that he frequently changed the position of his bed and had his sword and shield hung near to hand. I also heard that he slept soundly, but snored.

Henry's illegitimate daughters provided a route to the eventual submission of his brother, Robert. Their marriages strengthened his ties in France as he answered calls from his offspring for protection. Henry's constant proxy campaigning gave him the excuse to twice invade Normandy. The first time, he burned Bayeux to the ground, Caen switched sides in fear and he took Falaise. The second time, in

1106, he forced a final battle near Tinchebray Castle in which most of Robert's army was killed or captured. Robert Curthose was taken to Devizes Castle in England in the custody of bishop Roger of Salisbury where, I heard, he remains.

I saw Henry once more in the following year when he visited the new cathedral at Winchester. The main tower had fallen, the foundations unable to take the weight. I was summoned and found him in a series of arguments.

Someone blamed the accident on the impious William Rufus who was buried in the Cathedral. Another wondered whether the imprisonment of Robert Curthose was wrong in the sight of God. Here, we had a fallen tower and it was being blamed on two of his brothers. Henry responded angrily to accusations of cruelty:

> *I have not kept my brother in fetters like a captured enemy but have placed him as a noble pilgrim in a royal castle and have kept him well supplied with abundance of food and other comforts and furnishing of all kinds.*

Henry went with me down to the lady chapel in the crypt. He wanted someone to take responsibility for the collapse. I showed him how the damp was already at work and described the log foundations.

'The stone for the building came by water to Winchester from Quarr in the Isle of Wight,' I explained. 'A replacement tower will need large sub-structures and supports of unusual strength. I suspect the vaulting underneath and spanning the presbytery will need to be in wood, painted to look like stone. A spire would be highly desirable, but the cathedral may not be able to take the weight. The cost of work to date has taxed the full resources of both bishop and monastery. All in all, this building is a problem waiting for future generations.'

The king said a number of impious things.

'Money. It's always money. What do I do about that?'

'There is an answer,' I suggested. 'There has been quarrel after quarrel as bishop Giffard has sought to apply the full profit of Winchester Fair to the building. What I suggest is that you extend the fair on St Giles Hill considerably to make it even more successful. The resulting taxes will go a long way to fixing the problem as long as they do not build a heavy spire.

'Also, it's time to take down the New Minster. This will provide much needed stone and wood. There is a replacement site which has been discussed just outside the city at Hyde Mead to the north of the walls. It is not far from my home here.'

There were other advantages, I pointed out. The bodies of Alfred, his wife Ealhswith, and his son Edward the Elder could be moved there in a ceremony which would show respect for Saxon royalty, never a bad thing in times of healing.

'It will be a popular pilgrimage destination which will bring in more revenue.'

'I am in your debt again, Sir Gilbert. And, I will need leaders for Hyde. Let me take advice.'

Henry did take advice for, at the abbey's consecration in 1110, I watched the bodies of the Saxon royal family carried in state from the minster along my road and through the north gate to be received and interred before the high altar by the abbot, Geoffrey. By Geoffrey's side stood his newly welcomed cantor, my son, Andrew. Clearly, who you know always helps, but, to my direct question, I was assured that his appointment was made with the approval of Anselm just before his recent death in Canterbury. At the celebratory meal that afternoon, the abbot's praises for Andrew's intellectual devotion, scholarship and clarity of voice were widely discussed. Andrew, if he wishes, has a long career in the church. Ailgifu would have burst with pride.

Beekeeping is a little understood business. I had a good teacher, but in the last years, living mostly alone, I applied myself to the study of these worthy and industrious creatures. The great drawback is that, at harvest time, the whole colony is destroyed when the hive is smashed to remove the honey. This did not matter to wild hunter gatherers, but was destructive of income when one tried to run a business. Far more hives were needed than were really necessary.

I had been experimenting with movable comb boards in my hives to see if I could take one out when full without upsetting the bees. If I could do this, then the hives would not need to be destroyed. It was clear that the distance between the boards was important so that the bees had space to move around while they did their work, but close enough to maintain their sense of community. I had studied my copy of the rare *Geoponika*, given to me in happy times by Lēofric. Keepers in Egypt in antiquity blew smoke into their hives in order to calm their bees. Perhaps I could do this while taking a honeycomb out?

I tried many types of fuel for my smoking apparatus and found old rope the best for its slow burning and high levels of smoke if lit when damp. I put together a small bellows to inject the smoke into the hive.

My hives were made of wood with a door for a lid. They were stood against a wall twice their height which guarded them from high winds and the southern sun. I stood with a net of fine material over my head for protection against stings, my arms in long gloves and pushed smoke gently into a batch of four hives. I heard my name called. It was a man, probably near his forties, dressed in a monk's habit, riding a donkey. He carried the mark of a priest.

'Good lord, man, you look like some monster from the depths. What are you doing?'

I explained some of the mysteries of beekeeping. He listened, fascinated, and plied me with questions.

'It seems I have found Sir Gilbert of Bayeux-cum-Ropley,' he said. 'I have been recommended to you by your esteemed son, Andrew, the cantor of Hyde by Winchester. I am Orderic Vitalis of the abbey of Saint-Évroul near the River Orne in Normandy.'

Orderic explained that he was on a journey to pay homage at his father's grave at St Peter's abbey church in Shrewsbury. He had been sent as a boy to Saint-Évroul by his father who was priest to his sponsor, earl Roger of Montgomery.

'I must stop you there,' I said. 'I am an old man and have no wish to get involved any longer in Norman in-fighting. I know of the earl, who some say was lord of my wife's lands in the manor of Alresford. I also know some of his sons, particularly Robert of Bellême who was a most inconstant man and came with an army to this very place to try to steal England.'

'You need have no fear of me,' replied Orderic. 'I would use stronger language to describe Bellême. My intentions are innocent. I was able to visit Canterbury and decided to see Andrew in Winchester on my way to Shrewsbury. He is a man of great learning with an impressive understanding of the texts. You should be a proud father.'

Orderic explained his mission: 'I have recently finished interpolating a copy of William of Jumièges' *Gesta Normannorum ducum*, in which the writer tells the story from the conquest to the reign of Henry from the conqueror's viewpoint. My superiors have now ordered me to write the history of our abbey. I will do this, of course, but I intend it will grow into a many-volumed *Historia Ecclesiastica* which will tell the whole tale of the Normans as I see it. It is a peculiar honour, of course, as my father was English.

'My abbey is a house of wealth. War damaged knights use it as a resting pace for their last years. We have many visitors from the Christian world who bring me their stories. These events, I believe, are an expression of God's purpose. I would like your help by adding your experiences.'

'I am no longer interested in the history of those people,' I said ruefully. 'They have all caused me great pain. I do not wish to spend any time writing. I am more interested in my bees.'

'You have to do nothing,' said Orderic. 'Andrew tells me you have always written down your thoughts. You have been involved in many of the great events from Odo's time at Bayeux through the conquest to the embroidery which is now hanging in the cathedral there. You know of the lootings, of the Winchester Book, of the rebels, of the death of kings, of the changes in your city, to the battle that never happened at Alton.

'What I ask is to be your guest for the time it takes me to read what you have already written. You will inform my history. My history, I hope, before God, will inform the world.

'What do you say?'

It took Orderic three days to read my rude scraps. Often, he scribbled thoughts or copied segments onto his own parchment. Twice, he came to me with tears in his eyes and placed a hand on my shoulder, but said nothing. He asked no questions. At night, with our mead, we talked of other things.

Meantime, I worked with my bees and read those parts of *Geoponika* that offered guidance to me.

> *The bee is the wisest and cleverest of all animals and the closest to man in intelligence; its work is truly divine and of the greatest use to mankind. Its social life resembles that of the best-regulated cities. In their excursions bees follow a leader and obey instructions. They bring back sticky secretions from flowers and trees and spread them like ointment on their floors and doorways. Some are employed in making honey and some in other tasks.*
>
> *The bee is extremely clean, settling on nothing that is bad smelling or impure; it is not greedy; it will not approach flesh or blood or fat but only things of sweet flavour. It does not spoil the work of others, but fiercely defends its own work against those who try to spoil it. Aware of its own weakness, it makes the entrance to its home narrow and winding, so that those entering in large number to do harm are easily destroyed by the guardian bees ...*

This is the only animal that looks for a leader to take care of the whole community: it always honours its king, follows him enthusiastically wherever he goes, supports him when he is exhausted, carries him and keeps him safe when he cannot fly. It particularly hates laziness; bees unite to kill the ones who do no work and use up others' production.

When Orderic was finished, he came to me and we embraced for a long time.

'I am forever in your debt,' he announced. 'What I write will have so much more meaning.'

We discussed the bees as he packed his meagre belongings onto his donkey.

'I would like to do one thing as I leave,' he asked. 'I would like you to take me to Ailgifu's grave.'

We rode in silence to my favourite place in the world looking down on our hives at Ropley. We dismounted and he said the funeral prayers and blessed the spot. We embraced for one last time. He rode to the west to Shrewsbury.

AUTHOR'S EPILOGUE

Orderic Vitalis completed his eight-volume general history in 1142 when he was sixty-seven. It was his practice, following Gilbert, to place speeches into the mouths of the chief personalities in his stories in order to illustrate their character and policy. *Historia Ecclesiastica* is recognised today as the greatest English social history of the Middle Ages.[1]

There is no known record of when or where Gilbert died although I assume it was soon after his meeting with Orderic and at his home in the road in Ropley now called Gilbert Street. The name Gilbert was associated with the village for centuries.[2] Nor has any mention been found of the further career of his son, Andrew, the first cantor of Hyde Abbey.

King William's propensity for Ropley honey is noted in many local histories.[3] Three fields, East and West Honey Linch, together about ten acres, worked by Nicholas Mayhew, and Honey Linch, about twelve acres under John Eames Waight, are recorded in a list of life-hold lands of Ropley Manor, compiled between 1786 and 1788.[4] In a further Manor survey of 1811, three fields, East, Middle and West Honey Linch, had been passed by Mayhew to a Michael Rivers.[5]

The current *Castle of Comfort* in Castle Street, Medstead, is thought to be on or near Ailgifu's mead house. Its cockatrices were copied from Wherwell Abbey.[6] A house adjoining the hostelry sits above the mosaic floor of a Roman villa identified by an eyewitness during renovation.[7] The nearby hill fort is a scheduled monument and was surveyed in 1915 when much of the site was

1   See also: Chibnall, *The World of Orderic Vitalis*, 1984; Rozier, edited, *Orderic Vitalis, Life, Works and Interpretations*, 2016; Douglas, edited, *English Historical Documents 1042-1189*, 1953, for other interpretations.
2   'Parishes: Ropley', *A History of the County of Hampshire*, Vol. 3, 1908, p. 55.
3   www.ropley2000.hampshire.org.uk/index.htm.
4   Ropley Manor terrier, *Winchester College Archives*, 21412/40; transcribed Heal, *Ropley's Legacy*, Appendix 19, pp. 334-347.
5   *Winchester College Muniments*, 21413a.
6   www.hampshire-history.com/the-wherwell-cockatrice.
7   Private emails.

covered by thick undergrowth.[8] A small, stone Saxon coffin was unearthed in 1863 during the building of the railway line near *The Shant* public house close to where Gilbert buried Ailgifu.[9] It was examined by scientists from the Hartley Institution at Southampton. The coffin was moved to St Peter's, Ropley's parish church. Private metal detectorists have since found other dug and grave-shaped enclosures near by.[10]

Gilbert's Winchester home in Scowrtenestret, Shoemakers' Street, and later Gywerystrete, was frequently referred to as *Vicus Judeorum* or Jewry street from the 13th century.[11]

The portraits of Gilbert, Ailgifu and Lēofric can be found in the Bayeux Tapestry on display at its museum in France.[12] There are many competing theories on their significance.[13] The role of queen Edith and bishop Odo in the tapestry's creation has recently been rethought.[14] More recent research was added to Gilbert's account to describe the visit of the Tapestry to Geoffrey de Montbray's holdings at Bentworth.[15]

The confusion with the entry of the Ashley Hundred (Bishop's Sutton) and its ownership by Count Eustace of Bordeaux is discussed in most transcriptions of Domesday Book.[16]

The forged charter of the grant of king Ine to Winchester Cathedral is held in the *Codex Wintoniensis* at the British Library.[17]

---

8   www.historicengland.org.uk/listing/the-list/list-entry/1001920. Williams-Freeman, *An Introduction to Field Archaeology*, 1915, Part 2.

9   Mills, *Four Marks, its Life and Origins*, 1995, p. 7. Heal, *The Four Marks Murders*, second edition, Chapter 1, 'Racism and the coming of the railway', 2021.

10 Private emails.

11 www.wessexarch.co.uk/our-work/19-20-jewry-street-winchester.

12 www.bayeuxmuseum.com, Sheet 15.

13 For example, Messent, *The Bayeux Tapestry Embroiders' Story*, 1999, p. 65, and numerous internet theories.

14 Hicks, *The Bayeux Tapestry*, 2007, and Rowley, *The Man Behind the Bayeux Tapestry*, 2013.

15 Shore, 'Bentworth and its Historical Associations', 1897, and Patourel, 'Geoffrey of Montbray, Bishop of Coutances', 1944.

16 Munby, *Domesday Book, Hampshire*, 1982, p. 44 b and c and, especially, under 'Notes', p. 1. For entries for the ridge villages see Heal, *Ropley's Legacy*, Appendix 2, 2021, pp. 239-241. For an excellent overview, see Harvey, *Domesday, Book of Judgement*, 2014.

17 *British Library*, London, Additional Manuscript 15350, folios 20v-21r, Numbers 56 and 57 (s. xii); Birch 398; Kemble 1039; Sawyer 242. For a transcription and review, see Heal, *Ropley's Legacy*, Appendix 1, 2021, pp. 232-38. The charter contains the Saxon land boundaries used in this book. They are listed and discussed in detail within Grundy, 'Saxon Land Charters', 1921, pp. 69-78. Also, Langlands, *Ancient Ways of Wessex*, 2019, p. 82.

Gilbert's warnings over the dangerous foundations of Winchester Cathedral came to a head in 1906 when it was recognised that the building, sinking slowly into the ground, was in imminent danger of collapse. For five years until 1911, diver William Walker worked daily under water to a depth of twenty feet shoring up the building using more than 25,800 bags of concrete, 114,900 concrete blocks and 900,000 bricks.[18]

Before the Treaty of Alton (and Winchester), Gilbert was taken to meet Henry Beauclerc at a long barn house, imagined near to the River Itchen.[19] Other than Gilbert's account, details of the confrontation and negotiation at Alton in 1101 between the brothers Henry and Robert Curthose are sketchy in contemporaneous records.[20] The treaty, described in the *Anglo-Saxon Chronicle*, has been lost. Count Eustace, who declared for Robert Curthose, was the only noble mentioned as he sought to reclaim his English lands, including Sutton.

Gilbert's last great project, the first of the two major twelfth-century surveys of the borough of Winchester, the *Winton Domesday*, is now held in London.[21] Both surveys have been extensively investigated and combined with much recent archaeological work.[22]

After his capture at Tinchebray by Henry, his youngest brother, Robert Curthose remained incarcerated for twenty-eight years, the rest of his life. He died aged about eighty-four at Cardiff Castle in 1134.[23] Henry died the following year while on campaign in Normandy. He went to Lyons-la-Forêt to hunt where he ate a large serving of lampreys against doctor's orders, suffered an attack and was dead within a week. 'His death was a great shock as he had scarcely ever been sick and was a man of great vigour and energy.'[24]

Henry's marriage to queen Matilda of Scotland was a mostly successful union of the Anglo-Norman and Anglo-Saxon dynasties. Their only son, Winchester-

---

18 *Hampshire Observer*, 2 September 1911; Bussby, Frederick, *William Walker*, 1974; Henderson, Ian Thomson, *The Winchester Diver: The Saving of a Great Cathedral* (Henderson & Stirk, 1984); Duggan, Margaret, 'Diver who saved a cathedral', *Church Times*, 3 October 2006.

19 Fergie and Roberts, *Traditional Houses of the Worthy Villages*, 2020, pp. 10-12.

20 *The Anglo-Saxon Chronicle*, translated Garmonsway, 1953, pp. 236-38; translated Savage, 1982, pp. 240-41.

21 *Society of Antiquaries*, MS. 154.

22 Biddle, edited, *Winchester in the Early Middle Ages*, 1976.

23 Aird, *Robert Curthose*, 2008.

24 Hollister, *Henry I*, 2001, pp. 467-8.

born William Ætheling, died in the sinking of the *White Ship* in 1120. William's death left the succession of the English throne open to dispute.

On Henry's death, Stephen of Blois, the Conqueror's grandson through a daughter, Adela, quickly crossed the channel and claimed the throne aided by his brother, Henry of Blois, the bishop of Winchester.

Stephen remained king of England until 1154. Most of his reign was a bloody civil war in which he was challenged by his cousin, the empress Matilda, Henry's only legitimate surviving child. The period was known as the *Anarchy* for its widespread and lengthy breakdown of law and order.

GILBERT'S CHRONOLOGY

c. 1045   Birth

While working for Odo, bishop of Bayeux:

1050-58   Worked in kitchens at Bayeux

1059   Began training as a clerk

1064-66   Collected rents in Normandy

1066-67   Harbour Master for returning invasion fleet

     Registered loot from England

1067   Called to Winchester

     Took Lēofric as a servant

1067-68   Identified lands of thegns fallen at Hastings

1068   Argued against slavery

     Spy / messenger to queen Edith at Wilton

1069-71   Facilitated Bayeux embroidery

1070   Pleaded for the life of Kent, brother of Ailgifu

     Visited Old Sarum

1071   Attended archbishop Lanfranc's inaugural mass

     Visited bishop Stigand for a confession

1072   *Married Ailgifu at Medstead*

     Attended Stigand's funeral

     Watched return of body of Richard to Winchester

     Hearing and negotiations at Penenden Heath

     Commissioned by Lanfranc to assist with cathedral

     Altered and displayed embroidery at Bentworth

1073   Showed embroidery to Edith at Wilton

1075   *Birth of first child*

For Lanfranc, archbishop of Canterbury:

1076   Discovered watery foundation of cathedral

     Execution party for Waltheof at Winchester

1076-7   Clerk of works at Winchester Cathedral

For Odo, bishop of Bayeux

1081-82   Took messages to conspirators across England

For Hugh de Port, sheriff of Hampshire:

1082   Arrest guard for Odo in Freshwater, IoW

For Ranulf Flambard, tax collector:

1086   Helped organise national survey at Winchester

Attended the great oath of Sarum

Lessened value of Alresford in survey

1087   Watched arrival of William Rufus as king

For Walkelin, bishop of Winchester:

1087   Discussed church forgeries with abbot Scolland

Forged charters of Alresford's ownership

For Ranulf Flambard, tax collector:

1088   Watched Odo's rebellion

1093   Attended destruction of Old Minster

Death of three of his children

Collected rents

1095   Attended reading of pope Urban's call to crusade

Supported Lēofric on crusade

1096   Collected tax to fund Robert Curthose's crusade

1097   Diverted Winchester Fair rents to Walkelin

1100   Commemorated Lēofric at cathedral

Witnessed body of Rufus / attended burial

For Henry Beauclerc, king:

1101   Arrested for high treason

Death of Ailgifu

Adviser / negotiator at Battle of Alton

Requested law to abolish slave trade in England

1102   Commissioner for survey of king's land at Winchester

1107	Financial solution to the tower at Winchester Cathedral
1110	Advised using Hyde Abbey for Saxon royals
1111	*Son Andrew appointed cantor at Hyde*

For himself:

1112	Kept bees at Ropley
	Provided material for Orderic Vitalis's chronicle
By 1120	*Died, probably at Ropley*

READING LIST

Abulafia, Anna Sapir, and Evans, G. R., *The Works of Gilbert Crispin* (Oxford University Press 1986)

Aird, William M., *Robert Curthose, Duke of Normandy, c. 1050-1134* (Boydell Press, Woodbridge 2008)

Asbridge, Thomas, *The First Crusade, A New History* (Free Press, London 2005)

Barlow, Frank, *The Feudal Kingdom of England, 1042-1216* (1955; Longman, London 1977); *The English Church, 1000-1066: A history of the later Anglo-Saxon church* (1963; Longman, London 1979); *Edward the Confessor* (1970; Methuen, London 1989); *William Rufus* (1983; Yale University Press 2000)

Bates, David R., 'The Character and Career of Odo, Bishop of Bayeux', *Speculum*, Vol. 50, No. 1, January 1975, pp. 1-20; *William the Conqueror* (1989; History Press, Stroud 2008); 'The Forged Charters of William the Conqueror and Bishop William of St Calais', in Rollason, David W., Harvey, Margaret M., and Prestwich, Michael C., edited, *Anglo-Norman Durham 1093-1193* (Boydell Press, Woodbridge 1998), pp. 111-124

Biddle, Martin, edited, *Winchester in the Early Middle Ages, An Edition and Discussion of The Winton Domesday*, Winchester Studies 1 (Oxford University Press 1976); *The Search for Winchester's Anglo-Saxon Minsters* (Winchester Excavations Committee, Oxford 2018)

Bishop, T. A. M., and Chaplais, P., edited, *Facsimiles of English Royal Writs to A.D. 1100*, presented to Galbraith, Vivian Hunter (Oxford at the Clarendon Press 1957)

Blair, P. Hunter, *Anglo-Saxon England, An Introduction* (1959, Cambridge University Press 1977); *Roman Britain and Early England 55 BC - 871 AD* (Cardinal, London 1975)

Bolton, Timothy, *Cnut The Great* (Yale University Press, London 2017)

Borman, Tracy, *Matilda: Wife of the Conqueror; First Queen of England* (Vintage, London 2012)

Bowie, Gavin, 'Seorebryg to City of Seribury: an analysis of the period 1066-92', *Hampshire Field Club & Archaeological Society*, Newsletter No. 75, Spring 2021, pp. 2-4

Bridgeford, Andrew, *1066: The Hidden History of the Bayeux Tapestry* (Harper Perennial, London 2004)

Burchfield, Robert, *The English Language* (OUP 1986)

Chibnall, Marjorie, *The World of Orderic Vitalis, Norman Monks and Norman Knights* (Boydell Press, Woodbridge 1984); *The Ecclesiastical History of Orderic*

Vitalis, edited and translated (Oxford Medieval Texts, 1990); *The Normans* (Blackwell, Oxford 2000)

Clanchy, M. T., *England and its Rulers 1066-1772, Foreign Lordship and National Identity* (Fontana, London 1983); *Early Medieval England* (Folio Society, London 1997); *From Memory to Written Record, England 1066-1307* (Wiley-Blackwell, Chichester 2013)

Dalby, Andrew, translation, *Geoponika, Farm Work* (Prospect, London 2011)

Dennis, Christopher, 'The Career of Geoffrey de Montbray, Bishop of Coutances (1048-1093) and unus de primatibus Anglorum ('one of the chief men of the English')', unpublished PhD thesis, Cardiff University, 2012

Douglas, David C., and Greenaway, George W., edited, *English Historical Documents 1042-1189* (Eyre & Spottiswoode, London 1953), including, particularly, Tucker, Miss S. I., translation, *The Anglo-Saxon Chronicle, 1042-1154*; the *Annals of Florence of Worcester, 1042-1066*; William of Jumièges, *Description of the Invasion of England by William the Conqueror*, 7th Book, *Gesta Normannorum Ducum*; William of Poitiers, *The Deeds of William, duke of the Normans and king of the English*, c. 1071; Orderic Vitalis, *The Ecclesiastical History*, between 1123 and 1141; William of Malmesbury, *The Deeds of the Kings of the English* and *The Modern History* from the *Gesta Regum Anglorum* and the *Historia Novella*, between 1135 and 1142; and many others.

Dugdale, William, Dodsworth, Roger, edited, *Monasticon Anglicanum*, 2 vols (1655, 1661)

Dyer, Christopher, *Making a Living in the Middle Ages, The People of Britain 850-1520* (Yale, London 2002)

Edwards, Heather, 'The Charters of the Early West Saxon Kingdom', unpublished PhD thesis, University of Glasgow, 1985

Farmer, D. H., Bede, *The Ecclesiastical History of the English People* (Penguin, London 1990); *The Age of Bede* (Penguin, London 2004)

Fennell, Edward, *Charter for Murder* (Inserts Publishing, Winchester 2021)

Fergie, Bill, and Roberts, Edward, *Traditional Houses of the Worthy Villages* (Worthys Local History Group 2020)

Finn, R. Welldon, *The Domesday Inquest and the Making of Domesday Book* (Longmans, London 1966); *The Norman Conquest and its effects on the economy 1066-86* (Longmans, London 1971)

Fleming, Robert, *Kings and Lords in Conquest England* (Cambridge University Press 1995)

Galbraith, V. H., 'Royal Charters to Winchester', *The English Historical Review*, Vol. 35, No. 139, July 1920, pp. 382-400

Garmonsway, G. N., *The Anglo-Saxon Chronicle* (1953; Dent, London 1986)

Gibson, Margaret, *Lanfranc of Bec* (Clarendon Press, Oxford 1978)

Gillingham, John, *William II, The Red King* (Penguin, London 2019)

Grundy, George Beardoe, 'The Saxon Land Charters of Hampshire with Notes on Place and Field Names', *The Archaeological Journal*, No. 1, Vol. 83, 1921, pp. 55-173

Hall, J. R. Clark, *A Concise Anglo-Saxon Dictionary* (1894; University of Toronto Press 1960)

Hamer, Richard, edited, *A Choice of Anglo-Saxon Verse* (Faber and Faber, London 1970)

Harvey, Sally, *Domesday Book of Judgement* (Oxford University Press, 2014)

Hawkes, C. F. C., 'Old Roads in Central Hants', *Hampshire Field Club*, Vol. 9, Part 3, 1925, pp. 324-333

Heal, Chris, *Ropley's Legacy*, 'Grant of King Ine to Winchester Cathedral of land at Alresford, A.D. 701', Appendix 1 (Chattaway and Spottiswood, 2021)

Hicks, Carola, *The Bayeux Tapestry, The Life Story of a Masterpiece* (Vintage, London 2007)

Hollister, C. Warren, *The Making of England, 55 B.C. to 1399* (1966; Barnes & Noble, New York 1994); 'The Anglo-Norman civil war: 1101', *The English Historical Review*, Vol. LXXXVIII, Issue CCCXLVII, April 1973, pp. 315-354

John, Eric, 'Edward the Confessor and the Norman succession', *The English Historical Review*, No. CCCLXXI, April 1979, pp. 241-267

Keynes, Simon, edited, *Alfred The Great: Asser's Life of King Alfred and other Contemporary Sources* (Penguin, London 1983)

Kitchen, G. W., *Historic Towns: Winchester*, edited by Freeman, E. A. and Hunt, W. (Longmans, Green, London 1903)

Lack, Katherine, *Conqueror's Son, Duke Robert Curthose, Thwarted King* (History Press, Stroud 2018)

Langlands, Alexander, *The Ancient Ways of Wessex, Travel and Communications in an Early Medieval Landscape* (Oxbow Books, Oxford 2019)

Lavelle, Ryan, and Roffey, Simon, edited, *Danes in Wessex, The Scandinavian Impact on Southern England, c. 800-c. 1100* (Oxbow, Oxford 2016); and with Weikert, Katherine, *Early Medieval Winchester, Communities, Authority and Power in an Urban Space, c. 800-c. 1200* (Oxbow, Oxford 2021)

Levison, Wilhelm, *England and the Continent in the Eighth Century, The Ford Lectures, 1943* (Oxford at the Clarendon Press, 1946)

Magennis, Hugh, and Swan, Mary, edited, *A Companion to Ælfric* (Brill, Leiden 2009)

Malmesbury, William of, *The Deeds of the Bishops of England (Gesta Pontificum Anglorum)*, translated Prest, David (Boydell Press, Woodbridge 2002); *Chronicle of the Kings of England From the Earliest Period to the Reign of King Stephen*, translated Giles, J. A. (1847)

Maltby, M., *Feeding a Roman Town, Environmental evidence from excavations in Winchester, 1972-1985* (Hampshire Cultural Trust, Winchester Museums, 2010)

Messent, Jan, *The Bayeux Tapestry Embroiderers' Story* (Search Press, Tunbridge Wells 2010)

Mills, Betty, *Four Marks, its Life and Origins* (Repton Publishing, Four Marks 1995)

Morris, Marc, *The Anglo-Saxons, A History of the Beginnings of England* (Hutchinson, London 2021)

Munby, Julian, *Domesday Book, Hampshire* (Phillimore, Chichester 1982)

Neveux, François, *A Brief History of The Normans, The Conquests that Changed the Face of Europe* (Constable & Robinson, London 2006)

O'Brien, Bruce R., 'From Morðor to Murdrum: The Preconquest Origin and Norman Revival of the Murder Fine', *Speculum*, Vol. 71, No. 2, April 1996, pp. 321-357; 'Earls, ceorls, thegns and lords: English Society on the eve of the Conquest', downloaded January 2022, www.academia.edu

O'Brien, Harriet, *Queen Emma and the Vikings, The Woman Who Shaped the Events of 1066* (Bloomsbury, London 2006)

Oppenheimer, Stephen, *The Origins of the British* (Robinson, London 2007)

Óskarsdóttir, Svanhildur, *Egils' Saga* (Penguin, London 1997)

Ottaway, Patrick and Qualmann, Ken, *Winchester's Anglo-Saxon, Medieval and Later Suburbs, Excavations 1971-86* (Hampshire Cultural Trust, Winchester Museums, 2018)

Patourel, Le, John, 'Geoffrey of Montbray, Bishop of Coutances, 1049-1093', *The English Historical Review*, May 1944, Vol. 59, No. 234, pp. 129-161

Pelteret, David A. E., *Slavery in Early Medieval England from the Reign of Alfred until the Twelfth Century* (Boydell Press, Woodbridge 2001)

Poole, A. L., *Domesday Book to Magna Carta, 1087-1216* (Oxford History of England, second edition 1953)

Prestwich, J. O., 'The Career of Ranulf Flambard', in Rollason, David W., Harvey, Margaret M., and Prestwich, Michael C., edited, *Anglo-Norman Durham 1093-1193* (Boydell Press, Woodbridge 1998), pp. 299-310

Pryor, Francis, *Britain AD, A Quest for Arthur, England and the Anglo-Saxons* (Harper, London 2004)

Rathbone, Lorents, *Chronicle of Medstead* (1966, private, HRO, 32M 94/1/71)

Rees, H., Crummy, H., Ottaway, P. J., and Dunn, G., *Artefacts and Society in Roman and Medieval Winchester, Small finds from the suburbs and defences, 1971-1986* (Hampshire Cultural Trust, Winchester Museums, 2008)

Rex, Peter, *The English Resistance, The Underground War Against the Normans* (Amberley, Stroud 2014)

Richardson, H. G., *The Governance of Medieval England from the Conquest to Magna Carta* (Edinburgh at the University Press 1963)

Ronay, Gabriel, *The Lost King of England, The East European Adventures of Edward the Exile* (Boydell Press, Woodbridge 1989)

Rowley, Trevor, *The Man Behind the Bayeux Tapestry, Odo, William the Conqueror's Half-Brother* (History Press, Stroud 2013)

Rozier, Charles C., Roach, Daniel, Gasper, Giles E. M., and Van Houts, Elisabeth, editors, *Orderic Vitalis, Life, Works, Interpretations* (Boydell, Woodbridge 2019)

Rumble, Alexander Richard, 'The Structure and Reliability of the *Codex Wintoniensis*', unpublished PhD thesis, University of London, 1979

Samuels, Alec, 'The Death of King William II, William Rufus: Accident or Design?', *Hampshire Field Club & Archaeological Society*, Newsletter No. 75, Spring 2021, pp. 220-21

Savage, Anne, edited, *The Anglo-Saxon Chronicles* (Phoebe Phillips, London 1982)

Sawyer, Peter, edited, *Domesday Book, A Reassessment* (Edward Arnold, London 1985); *The Wealth of Anglo-Saxon England* (Oxford University Press 2013)

Searle, Eleanor, 'Battle Abbey and Exemption: The Forged Charters', *The English Historical Review*, July 1968, Vol. 83, No. 238, pp. 449-480

Serjeantson, D., and Rees, H., *Food, Craft, and Status in Medieval Winchester, The plant and animal remains from the suburbs and city defences* (Hampshire Cultural Trust, Winchester Museums, 2009)

Shurlock, Barry, *The Winchester Story* (Milestone Publications, Horndean 1986)

Smith, Donald, *Old Furniture & Woodwork, An Introductory Historical Survey* (Batsford, London 1937)

Southern, R. W., 'Ranulf Flambard and Early Anglo-Norman Administration', *Transactions of the Royal Historical Society*, 1933, Vol. 16, pp. 95-128; *The Making of the Middle Ages* (1953; Hutchinson, London 1978)

Stafford, Pauline, *Queen Emma & Queen Edith, Queenship and Women's Power in Eleventh-Century England* (Blackwell, Oxford 2004)

Stenton, Sir Frank, *Anglo-Saxon England* (1943; OUP 1971, third edition)

Tatton-Brown, Tim, 'Recent Fieldwork around Canterbury', *Archaeologia Cantiana*, 99, 1983, pp. 115-132

Thirsk, Joan, edited, *Land, Church, and People, Essays presented to Professor H. P. R. Finberg* (Museum of English Rural Life, Reading 1970)

Qualmann, Ken, Scobie, Graham, and Zant, John, *Excavations at Hyde Abbey, Winchester, 1972-99* (Hampshire Cultural Trust, Winchester Museums, 2010)

Videen, Hana, *The Word Hord, Daily Life in Old English* (Profile Books, London 2021)

Vitalis, Orderic, *The Ecclesiastical History Of England and Normandy*, translated Forester, Thomas (1114-1141; Bohn, London 1854; Forgotten Books eprint 2016)

Wace, Master, trans. Taylor, Edward, *His Chronicle of the Norman Conquest from the Roman de Rou* (1160; CreateSpace 2022)

Ward, Gordon, 'Forged Anglo-Saxon Charters', *Kent Archaeological Society*, 2017, pp. 147-152

Willis, The Reverend R., *The Architectural History of Winchester Cathedral* (1846; The Friends of Winchester Cathedral 1984)

Wood, Michael, *In Search of the Dark Ages* (BBC, London 2005)

INDEX OF PRINCIPAL CHARACTERS

Other books by Chris Heal

All books available through a variety of sellers described on www.candspublishing.org.uk: selected Hampshire retailers, major internet booksellers and direct from the publisher.

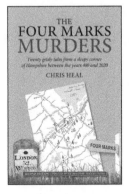

The first two books in the Ridge Trilogy

The Four Marks Murders (2020): Twenty grisly tales from a sleepy corner of Hampshire between the years 400 and 2020 (second edition updated with readers' suggestions)

In this true-life thriller, Chris Heal investigates deliberate and untimely deaths in what was thought to be one of the quiet backwaters of Hampshire. The murders begin in Roman times with over half since 1900 and three within the last few years and beg the question, 'Is Four Marks the murder capital of Southern England?'

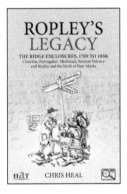

Ropley's Legacy (2021): The Ridge Enclosures, 1709 to 1850: Chawton, Farringdon, Medstead, Newton Valence and Ropley and the birth of Four Marks

The very first private parliamentary enclosure in England was in 1709 in Ropley. Driven by the less than saintly bishop of Winchester, it was a highly contested land grab seeking to make money by taking control of the common fields. Over 150 years the government sanctioned theft spread to all the neighbouring ridge villages.

The Sound of Hunger (2018)
An acclaimed social biography of two brothers, Georg and Erich Gerth, WW1 u-boat captains, set against Germany's political and militaristic development from Bismarck to Hitler.

Disappearing (2019)
A nomad with many names. A violent past. Infuriated by petty bureaucracy and the surveillance society. Determined to throw off identity and to leave no trace.

Reappearing (2020)
If an elderly couple save you from a bad death in the Sahara, there's an honest debt to be paid. But this couple have other plans. The only escape is down the River Niger.